DATE DUE

FEB 16 1994	
MAR 01 1994	
MAR 15 1994	Nakusp Public
MAR 29 1994	due Jan 2/01
OCT 13 1994	Burnaby Public
NOV 10 1994	due Mar 1/01
NOV 30 1994	DEC 12 2001
FEB 24 1995	MAR 25 2002
SEP 26 1995	OCT 31 2002
OCT 27 1995	DEC 07 2002
MAR 20 1996	NOV 19 2003
APR 2 1996	Richmond Public
	due Mar 7/04
NOV 28 1996	
MAR - 4 1997	
JAN 27 1998	

HYPNOSIS
AND THE
TREATMENT
OF DEPRESSIONS

Strategies for Change

Also by Michael D. Yapko, Ph.D.

FREE YOURSELF FROM DEPRESSION

TRANCEWORK
*An Introduction to the
Practice of Clinical Hypnosis*

WHEN LIVING HURTS
Directives for Treating Depression

BRIEF THERAPY APPROACHES FOR
TREATING ANXIETY AND DEPRESSION (*Ed.*)

HYPNOTIC AND STRATEGIC INTERVENTIONS
Principles and Practice (Ed.)

HYPNOSIS
AND THE
TREATMENT
OF DEPRESSIONS

Strategies for Change

MICHAEL D. YAPKO, Ph.D.

BRUNNER/MAZEL *Publishers* • NEW YORK

Dedicated with love to my wife, Diane,
for all the best reasons imaginable.

Library of Congress Cataloging-in-Publication Data
Yapko, Michael D.
  Hypnosis and the treatment of depressions : strategies for change
Michael D. Yapko.
    p.   cm.
  Includes bibliographical references and index.
  ISBN 0-87630-682-2 (hardbound)
  1. Depression, Mental—Treatment.   2. Hypnotism—Therapeutic use.
I. Title.
  [DNLM: 1. Depressive Disorder—therapy.   2. Hypnosis—methods.
WM171 Y25h]
RC537.Y354   1992
616.85′270651—dc20
DNLM/DLC
for Library of Congress   92-17478
                                                                          CIP

Published by
BRUNNER/MAZEL, INC.
19 Union Square West
New York, New York 10003

Manufactured in the United States of America

10 9 8 7 6 5 4 3 2 1

Contents

Tables

Foreword

What is the most ambiguous stimulus any of us ever face? What is so amorphous that it becomes whatever we make it out to be? As far as I can tell, the answer to those questions is LIFE! Life is an ambiguous stimulus, just like those inkblots you studied during your clinical training. Life is an experiential Rorschach! Life does not have any inherent meaning; it simply offers us opportunities to project onto it whatever matters to each of us based on our own unique backgrounds and makeup.

Some projections make us feel great: "Life is meant to be enjoyed to the fullest, using each precious moment to revel in the beauty of the world." Some projections make us feel terrible: "Life is a bitch, and then you die." Such negative views have a great deal to do with clinical depression—a disorder featuring an intricate system of negative projections about self, life, the universe—most *everything*. Knowing that these views are arbitrary, and therefore malleable, has a great deal to do with hypnosis, a field that has a better-than-average grasp of the complex notion that "reality" is essentially a subjectively created and experienced phenomenon.

This book breaks new ground, formally bringing together depression as a problem and hypnosis as a solution. It is a pairing of problem and treatment that is long overdue. Older conceptions about both depression and hypnosis that are now obsolete prevented such a union for a variety of reasons that will be described in detail. In short, hypnosis was viewed as a probable path to psychosis, hysteria, and even suicide if used with depressed individuals. But here is a whole new realm in which superstition can be replaced with fact. Hypnosis is broadly defined here as a model of influential communication. By defining hypnosis in this way, the rigid boundaries separating hypnosis as a distinct form of treatment from other therapeutic approaches are purposely weakened. The goal is to high-light the view that hypnotic patterns are evident in *all* therapies in order to encourage greater familiarity with and acceptance of hypnosis as a vital tool in treatment.

Recent epidemiological studies tell us what we probably already know—the rate of depression in this country (and other Western societies) is rising. The decline of the traditional nuclear family, changing roles of men and women, increased mobility (and therefore isolation), deemphasis on tradition, disillusionment with leaders of government and religious institutions, increases in crime, cultural emphasis on materialism and individualism, and a host of other socio-cultural changes have created a perfect climate for depression. Unless our fundamental views about depression change and the mental health profession gives the problem the prompt and serious attention it deserves, it saddens me to say that the rate of depression will, without a doubt, increase.

It was my intention in writing this book to take a fresh look at depression and to reconsider some of the "conventional wisdom" that has dominated the clinical treatment literature. Our knowledge of depression has dramatically improved in the past few years, render-ing obsolete many of the beliefs commonly held about its etiology and course. As a result, the essential role of psychotherapy has been firmly established as *vital*—not only to overcome episodes of depression, but also to minimize the likelihood of later relapses. Whenever psychotherapy is indicated, so are specific identifiable patterns of hypnotic influence, since the two are fundamentally inseparable.

The old myth of hypnosis stripping away a client's defenses or otherwise rendering him or her powerless is the virtual opposite of the empowerment that well-considered hypnosis can afford the client. I use the term "empowerment" quite deliberately, for it is both the core of hypnotic approaches and the inevitable goal in treating depressed individuals. Perhaps the word has become so common that it is almost a cliché, yet it remains an accurate representation of the nature of the therapeutic work described herein.

Over the past decade, I have focused almost exclusively on the problem of major depression. Specifically, I have been involved in analyzing a variety of treatment data in an effort to clarify what depression is and what to do about it. In accepting this challenge, my detailed knowledge of clinical hypnosis has given me a unique vantage point from which to view the experience of depression. I have developed a number of insights into the treatment of depressed clients, some of which may clarify aspects of proven therapy processes, whereas others may be contrary to methods that many therapists now routinely employ in their treatment of depressed individuals.

It is more accurate to talk about depressions than to consider major depression as if it were a singular entity, since it takes many different forms—almost as many as there are individual sufferers. What sometimes fools clinicians into a misdiagnosis is how frequently clients who evidence depression do not report feeling depressed. The person may complain of aimlessness, apathy, relationship problems, a tendency to drink too much, an upset stomach, or any of a thousand other things, and never mention a problem with mood.

Just what is depression? Although the DSM-III-R officially categorizes major depression as a mood disorder, clearly it is much more than that. I prefer to think of *depression as a life-style*, systemically encompassing all dimensions of a person's experience, including physiology, patterns of thought, relationship patterns, situational responses, and emotional and behavioral manifestations. It is a mistake to think of depression as only a prolonged but transient period of sadness or feeling bad. It involves too many enduring patterns that, left untreated, can keep even the fully recovered client at risk for later depressive episodes. *By the time a person becomes depressed, the life-style patterns that provided the foundation for the depression have long been in place; it is these long-standing patterns that we need to address.*

In 1988, *When Living Hurts: Directives for Treating Depression* was published, in which I detailed 91 directives that could be used in the treatment of depressed individuals, each addressing a different aspect of common depressive patterns. The present companion volume complements that earlier work by providing a more formal review of the current understanding of both hypnosis and depression, and elaborating on the theme that therapy is most effective with this disorder when it *actively* reshapes the way in which the client perceives and responds to life experience. Depression is highly treatable; with old myths out of the way, urgently needed treatment tools can become available. And hypnosis is a particularly valuable tool, as you will discover.

There are a great deal of data that show that depression responds remarkably well to brief, active, and directive therapy approaches. The role of experiential learning as a core element of such treatment methods has been firmly established; likewise, hypnosis as a vehicle for experiential learning is equally well established. The emphasis in this book, then, is on ways to create, recognize, and use opportunities to impart the specific learnings necessary to help a depressed client recover as quickly as possible and with minimal risk for future depressive episodes.

It is a fundamental truth that anything that has the ability to help also has the ability to hurt. What has become all too clear is that well-intentioned, but misdirected, therapy can aggravate a client's depressed condition. I hope that the ideas and techniques presented here will ultimately help to make treatment more effective. Depression is highly responsive to good therapy.

—MICHAEL D. YAPKO, PH.D.
San Diego, California

Acknowledgments

Always first and foremost, I want to express my deep appreciation to my wife, Diane, for her unwavering love and support for all I do.

Linda Griebel, who organizes and runs much of my daily professional life, deserves a great deal of credit for helping make this project run so smoothly.

Suzi Tucker, my editor at Brunner/Mazel, did a fantastic job of tightening up the manuscript and making it both more readable and accurate in representing my views.

John Koriath and Lynn Johnson, valued friends and esteemed colleagues, took the time to review the manuscript and provide critical feedback. Their comments were most useful and appreciated.

While there are professional colleagues and friends too numerous to name here, who directly and indirectly contributed ideas and support for this work, I would especially like to acknowledge the following people for their valuable input in the development of many of my ideas: Stephen Gilligan, Aaron T. Beck, Martin E. P. Seligman, Norma and Phil Barretta, Brian Alman, and Mark Tracten.

I want to thank my clients, who continue to inspire and amaze me with the profound lessons they teach.

I want to acknowledge with love Wendy and Richard Horowitz for being the best of friends, always providing love, support, and safe haven, both when everything is great and when times get tough.

I also want to express love and thanks to my family, a very loyal and loving bunch, who make me feel very lucky for what I have.

Finally, I want to acknowledge Megan Leigh Horowitz, Samuel Steven Wittenberg, and Zoe Isabelle Ross-Gilligan. You have done more to build expectancy than any therapist possibly could.

Introduction

Good therapy occurs in many ways. Consider for example, the case of the "African violet lady of Milwaukee." Reported by Erickson (in Zeig, 1980a), it involved a 52-year-old wealthy spinster, who lived alone in her big house in Milwaukee. She was horribly isolated and depressed, venturing out only to attend church services. Her depression worsened to the point that her nephew, a physician who knew Erickson, feared she would commit suicide. He asked Erickson to visit the woman during an upcoming trip to Milwaukee in the hope of somehow helping her.

Erickson arranged to meet the woman in her home. From talking with her and touring her home, he observed that: (1) she was isolated and depressed, with a passive and obedient interpersonal style; (2) she had a deep sense of commitment to her church community (even though she didn't actively participate in it); and (3) she grew some beautiful African violet plants. True to his utilization approach to therapy (described well in this book), Erickson grew curious about how the latter two values might be used to move the woman out of her depression.

He got the woman to agree to raise many more African violets. He then directed her to give one of these plants to a person or family in her church community each time an important traditional event occurred, such as a birth, illness, marriage, death, and so on. As Erickson reported, she followed these instructions and became "too busy to be depressed." Further, she became quite active in the community, and she earned the appreciation and attention of many people. In fact, when she died over 20 years later, she was mourned and lovingly remembered as the "African Violet Queen of Milwaukee."

What is remarkable to me about this case is how Erickson appreciated the woman in terms of her entire life space. He saw her as a unique person with many distinct values and interests. Although he recognized and addressed her depression, he did not define or reduce her to this or any other diagnostic label. He demonstrated that while persons stuck in problems typically restrict their attention (and hence their experience) to within the problem frame, therapists searching for solutions must widen their lens to include the many other aspects of the person. This can be difficult, for such information often is not given in the person's presentation; however, it is essential if the person is to get back to playing with a full deck in the game of life. Therapy becomes the art of shifting attention to include, incorporate, and integrate these additional values in the service of generating new possibilities for living.

It is this tradition initiated by Milton Erickson that Michael Yapko further develops in the present groundbreaking book. Whereas most therapists pay lip service to the idea that each client is first and foremost a person (rather than a diagnostic category), Yapko actually seems to believe and practice it. He emphasizes that because individuals are so diverse, therapy approaches must be flexible and individualized. He eschews monolithic explanations or formulaic methods in favor of tailored approaches that respect a person's reality while convincing him or her to expand it. He shares his considerable expertise about depression in a way that doesn't leave us feeling depressed! In fact, he gives considerable hope that a responsible therapist really can make a significant difference with folks suffering from depression. That in itself is a major contribution to our field.

I applaud and admire Yapko's courage in challenging the orthodoxy regarding the use of hypnosis in treating depression. In reviewing and refuting those that insist that hypnosis is dangerous with depressives, he cogently dispels erroneous views about both hypnosis and depression. He rightly criticizes the traditional understanding of hypnosis as a rigid set of communications that involve the performance of therapist-defined tasks, letting go of internal processes, and acceptance of therapist ideas that may be unrelated or even contradictory to the client's own ideas. If this were the only way hypnosis could be used, it would be inappropriate for many clients, not just depressives! The alternative approach to hypnosis espoused by Yapko is one that makes room for whatever the client is experiencing in a way that allows new experiences to develop. He describes how the meaning of hypnotic experience varies with context; it has no

inherent value. Thus, hypnosis may be helpful, harmful, or irrelevant, depending on how, where, when, and by whom it is being used.
In delineating these contextual variables, Yapko illustrates many
helpful ways in which hypnosis can be used in treating depression.

I believe this is the first book that address how hypnosis may be
helpful with depression. This alone makes it noteworthy. Just as significant, however, is that it leaves one with a much greater appreciation of both hypnosis and depression, and how the former might
be used to treat the latter. I hope you will find as much value in reading it as I did.

—STEPHEN GILLIGAN, PH.D.
Encinitas, California

HYPNOSIS
AND THE
TREATMENT
OF DEPRESSIONS

Strategies for Change

1

Depressions

The use of hypnosis as a therapeutic tool in the treatment of depression has been discouraged—both passively and actively—over the years. The reasons for this will be considered in depth in the next chapter. However, it must be emphasized at the outset that the fact is that the field of hypnosis provides many remarkable insights into the highly subjective realm of human experience. And since depression is a human condition rooted in subjectivity, increasing one's level of objectivity about life experience should be a core component of effective treatment (Beck, 1967; 1973; Ellis, 1979; 1987).

With hypnosis so clearly capable of altering subjective experience—one's interpretation of and response to life events—why isn't it used as a primary treatment tool in facilitating recovery from depression? The answer, in a general sense, stems from how hypnosis has been both misconceived and misapplied, rather than from its inherent nature.

This book encourages, and even demands, a reconsideration of what we know, or think we know, about hypnosis and about depression. When our desire is to help suffering individuals, it is simply too self-limiting to preclude the use of such a powerful treatment tool on the basis of outdated theories and techniques. Much has changed in the past few years regarding our understanding of hypnotic phenomena and of the nature of depression. It is my aim to help establish hypnosis as a viable, perhaps even necessary, component of effective treatment.

But first as a starting point for the ideas and methods to be presented later, we must go back to a description of the epidemiology of depression.

A PROBLEM ON THE RISE

Epidemiological data indicate quite clearly that despite the greater attention being given to mental health issues, despite the proliferation of countless approaches to psychotherapy, and despite advances in medical and psychological technologies for intervening, the rate of depression continues to increase (Charney & Weissman, 1988; Weissman, 1987; Klerman, 1988). Given this marked increase in depression, particularly in the last four or five decades, it seems eminently logical to ask these questions: Why is there so much depression today? What can mental health professionals do to provide more reliable and effective treatment for those individuals who are either depressed or at risk for depression? And only by asking further questions can we define an area of intensive study in an effort to obtain relevant answers. So, we may ask, "Could there be some new or preexisting, but dormant biological factor that would account for the increased rate of depression? Are there cultural or sociological explanations for its increase?"

CROSS-CULTURAL CONSIDERATIONS

One way to determine whether a problem is more biologically or more psychosocially influenced is to consider comparative data obtained in other cultures. In the case of depression, a considerable number of cross-cultural studies suggest that not only the prevalence of depression, but even the manner in which it is manifested, is influenced powerfully by cultural factors. In fact, the differences in the symptom patterns of depression between cultures, especially Western versus non-Western, are so great that some experts wonder whether it is even the same disorder under consideration (Marsella, 1979). This is the basis for my talking about depressions rather than depression as a well-defined, singular entity. (For the sake of readability, though, I generally use the term depression.)

In one example, anthropologist Edward Schiefflin (1985) studied the primitive (by Western definition) Kaluli tribe in New Guinea. According to Schiefflin, it appears that the incidence of clinical depression among the Kaluli is nearly zero. He described them individually as highly expressive emotionally and the tribe as largely community-based, with an emphasis on strong social ties among tribal members that is likely to minimize any personal sense of isolation or alienation. If one person has a grievance against another for some perceived wrong, the complainant is heard and responded to quickly, thus cutting down on the chances for feelings of isolation, hopelessness, and helplessness to arise.

Janice Egeland and Abram Hostetter, in their studies of the Old Order Amish in Pennsylvania, found that the rate of major depression (unipolar disorder) among them was somewhere between one fifth and one tenth that of the rest of the U. S. population (Egeland & Hostetter, 1983). Here, too, is a society that places a premium on family and community ties and stability of experience over time, that is, tradition. It is a society that shuns advanced technology and resists assimilation with others.

Other cultures show marked differences in the way life experience is interpreted and responded to, leading to a broad range in the rate of clinical depression, and in how the depression is manifested. For example, in China, the rate of depression appears to be close to that of the United States. Yet, it would be atypical for a Chinese person to complain of depression. Instead, he or she would be likely to complain of physical aches and pains (Kleinman, 1982). Similar somatization patterns for manifesting depression are found in many non-Western cultures (Marsella, Sartorius, Jablensky, & Fenton, 1985).

DEPRESSION AS A LEARNED PHENOMENON

The very fact that the rate of depression has steadily increased over the past 40 to 50 years (Sartorius & Ban, 1986; Seligman, 1988) suggests that some significant changes must have taken place in society during this time. In general, gene pools and biochemistry simply do not change that dramatically in such a short period. This is not to say that genetics and biochemistry do not play a role in depression; clearly, they do (Bertelsen, 1988; Willner, 1985). However, based on the epidemiological studies, the cross-cultural data, and the psychological research, it is apparent that most depressions are a product of experience, not biology (Brown, 1985; Brown & Harris, 1978; Dean, 1985; Seligman, 1990).

Still, it is evident that some forms of depression are the result of biological variables. If we consider that there are scores of diseases, as well as many medications, that have depression as a predictable side effect, or if we think about what is known about the seasonal affective disorder, it becomes clear that biology can play an important role in depression (Reich, VanEerdewegh, Rice, Mullaney, Endicott, & Klerman, 1987; Davis & Maas, 1983). However, it is important in diagnosing and treating depression to distinguish between biological *causes* and biological *correlates,* a distinction that has not yet been well made in the literature. The result has been a schism between those who take an exclusively biological view and those who take an exclusively psychosocial view of the origin and treatment of depression (Willner, 1985). I prefer a "both/and" perspective to an "either/or" view.

There is no reliable test to determine whether a depression is biologically based. Historically, when a patient demonstrated physiological symptoms of depression, or manifested depression in the absence of any clearly identifiable external stressors, the depression was assumed to be "endogenous" or biological in nature. Now it seems that such a narrow—and unprovable—approach may not always be a useful one for either diagnosing or treating the most salient dimensions of depression. The treatment data support this contention. Treatments of an exclusively biological nature, most notably antidepressant medications, unquestionably have demonstrated an ability to reduce symptoms of depression rapidly, and even to provide full recovery from depressive episodes. However, when the therapeutic intervention is solely a course of antidepressant medication, the relapse rate is significantly higher than when the depressed individual receives effective psychotherapy, either alone or in conjunction with drug treatment (Weissman, 1983; Becker & Heimberg, 1985; McGrath, Keita, Strickland, & Russo, 1990).

Studies indicate that an exclusively biological approach to the diagnosis and treatment of depression is not sufficient and may, in fact, be antitherapeutic in the long run (Akiskal, 1985; Weissman, 1983). If a depressed individual does not receive psychotherapy, and is more prone to relapses as a result, this would suggest that the relevant aspects of the person's depression have not been adequately addressed. Furthermore, the unwitting reinforcement in our drug-seeking society that drugs are the answer may actually work against real recovery. Is just a coincidence that the marked increase in the rate of depression in recent decades parallels the increased societal emphasis on the use—and abuse—of drugs?

It is especially interesting that the epidemiological data show a particularly significant increase in the rate of depression among those born since 1945, the so-called "baby-boomers" (Klerman, 1988; Weissman, 1987). In writing about this trend, noted psychologist Martin E. P. Seligman (1988, 1990) contended that the baby-boomers' high level of self-absorption and unrealistically high expectations fueled their higher rate of depression. Seligman's views reflect an awareness of the shifting cultural values that predispose individuals to depression. If we use the situation of the baby-boomers as a lens through which to examine the issue of *depression as a learned phenomenon,* we may be able better to determine the reason for today's high rate of depression.

WHAT CAUSES DEPRESSION?

Although depression has been described in countless ways throughout history, it has only been described meaningfully in the clinical literature for less than a century. The earliest attempts to explain who became depressed and why were steeped in abstract concepts and vague language that involved speculations about ambiguous personality constructs and hypothetical psychodynamics. Until recently, many of these earliest conceptions and their associated techniques went unchallenged and unclarified. The notion of depression as "anger turned against the self," for example, was not originated by Freud, but he certainly popularized it (Arieti & Bemporad, 1978). This view dominated the clinical literature as the "proper" conceptual framework for understanding depression. Its noncritical acceptance would suggest that clinicians sometimes devote themselves to a theoretical model that may have little relationship to the actual nature of a disorder. What we have learned in recent years is that depression is *not exclusively* a biological illness; neither can it be understood only as anger turned inward, a reaction to loss, a condition that exists because the person is rewarded for it through secondary gain, or something the client wants to experience. Each perspective may hold true in some cases; but none of them represents the essence of the disorder. Rigid viewpoints of depression that emphasize a specific psychodynamic or behavioral contingency have proved to be so limited as to be potentially destructive frameworks for attempting diagnosis and treatment (Akiskal, 1985; McGrath et al., 1990; Yapko, 1988).

Emerging in the treatment literature in recent years has been a shift away from abstract issues of a person's life in favor of a focus on specific patterns the individual uses in organizing and responding to his or her perceptions of life (deShazer, 1991; Fisch, Weakland & Segal, 1983). Epidemiological, cross-cultural, and treatment studies have fostered a clear recognition that any of a variety of patterned ways of responding to life circumstances can lead to the phenomenological experience of depression. Thus, there is no single cause for depression—there are many.

What are these various depressogenic patterns that one learns and from where or whom does one learn them? The patterns that place a person at risk for episodes of depression are drawn from a variety of sources that can be broadly categorized as cultural, familial, and individual.

Cultural Influences

In recognizing the marked increase, perhaps as much as tenfold, in the prevalence of depression among baby-boomers as compared with their parents' and grandparents' generations (Seligman, 1988; Robins, Helzer, Weissman, Orvaschel, Gruenberg, Burke, & Regier, 1984), the suggestion is strong that cultural climate and social milieu play a significant etiological role. Whereas gene pools and biochemistry are unlikely to change so radically in such a short time, a culture *can* go through swift and dramatic changes almost overnight. Perhaps the most obvious examples are primitive cultures that have been contaminated by Western influences (Marsella et al., 1985). But even our own culture has undergone extraordinary changes in the post-World War II years. It is, of course, possible to fill volumes describing these extraordinary sociological changes, but I will focus on some of those that I consider to have the greatest impact on the escalating rates of depression. (It should be noted that these are not discussed in any particular order.)

1. Breakdown of family relationships.

In 1960, when John F. Kennedy ran for the presidency, the fact that he was Roman Catholic emerged as a volatile campaign issue. During that more conservative period in American history, it was hazardous for a presidential candidate to be a member of what the public considered the "wrong" religion. At that time, had Kennedy been divorced, rather than a "stable family man," he simply could not have been elected. Twenty years later, when Ronald Reagan was a candidate for president, it was rarely, if ever, mentioned that he had been divorced. Would Reagan have been able to win the presidency if he had run 20 years earlier? One can speculate with a reasonable degree of certainty that his marital history would have been a target for criticism, and even used as an indicator of his (questionable) emotional stability.

Isn't it remarkable how in just 20 years, divorce has gone from being a relatively taboo practice to being widely accepted. What happened in the American psyche that led us not only to tolerate, but even to encourage, the breakup of marriages and families (Goldenberg & Goldenberg, 1985; Walsh, 1982)? Is it significant that most American families are no longer of the traditional nuclear type, but are blended families and single-parent families? It is true that in the psychological literature, the breakdown of the family is blamed for most of our problems, both as individuals and as a family. However, in the case of depression, at least, it is entirely appropriate that we consider the negative influences of the disintegration of family relationships.

The breakup of the family results not only from divorce, but also from geographical separation. In the absence of ongoing regular contact with family members, the necessary social skills that such intimacy engenders (e.g., tolerance, communication, conflict management, sharing), are sorely lacking. It is clearly a statement about American culture that relationships are as troubled as they are. Dating relationships are largely brief and unsatisfying. Those who want to have relationships do not seem to know where or how to meet others. What other culture encourages the seeking of dates through classified ads?

When families break up, children are especially likely to personalize the occurrence as evidence of their own lack of worth (Lefrancois, 1986). In fact, the divorcing partners may also conclude that the problems are personal, rather than interpersonal or situational. One's outlook on relationships and one's skill in obtaining and maintaining them are significant factors in the experience of depression, and there are numerous studies that reinforce this contention (Charney & Weissman, 1988; Beach, Nelson, & O'Leary, 1988). In at least 50 percent of those couples presenting for marital therapy, one or both partners are depressed and often other family members are as well. The reverse is also true: of those individuals presenting as clinically depressed, at least 50 percent are manifesting marital and/or family dysfunctions (Rounsaville, Weissman, Prusoff, & Herceg-Baron, 1979; Weissman, 1987; Beach, Sandeen, & O'Leary, 1990).

We have long known that relationships serve as a buffer against illness—either physical or mental (DiMatteo & Hays, 1981; Lin & Dean, 1984). In fact, when we look at the demographic data regarding who is most likely to become depressed, the highest risk category is found to be single women and the lowest risk category to be married men (Klerman, 1988). The evidence also suggests that the highest likelihood of relapse of depressive episodes is among individuals who continue in marital (and family) relationships characterized by poor communication, criticism and other verbal abuse, and lack of emotional support (Jacobson, 1985; Birtchnell, 1991). Thus, the evidence is overwhelming for a systemic approach to depression that involves partners and families in the treatment process when appropriate.

The key point is that relationships play a very large role in the experience of depression. Our cultural emphasis on isolation through divorce, frequent job changes, and geographical relocation is likely to continue to impair our ability to build the kinds of high-quality relationships that might help serve as buffers against depression.

2. The ambiguity of gender and other identity roles.

The concept of androgyny was touted at one time as a means to promote equality between the sexes by blurring the boundaries in traditional roles. Whether such blurring is desirable is not relevant here. What *is* relevant is that as gender roles have gone from being clearly delineated, almost scripted, to being vague and uncertain, there has been a double consequence. For those who can tolerate ambiguity well (who, in fact, are less prone to depression), the ambiguity of gender roles has not posed any significant problems. However, for those individuals who do not tolerate ambiguity well, the uncertainty of what is appropriate to expect of oneself based on one's maleness or femaleness, or the blurring of traditional gender roles, has led to significant emotional distress. For such people, it no longer is clear as to who does what in a relationship, thus creating further confusion about discrepancies between expectations and reality. Furthermore, as the role of women in the work force continues to increase, more and more households have dual incomes, which creates the potential for greater material gain. Thus, simultaneously, gender roles have become unclear and an emphasis on materialism has emerged.

The frustration arising from a lack of clear definitions of appropriate gender behavior, and, therefore, of appropriate behavior in many interpersonal contexts (business, family, etc.), is a predictable consequence of the diversity of views in our culture. The confusion beomes manifest as double standards for men and women in such areas as financial equity and sexual behavior. Many respond to that confusion with depression (Wetzel, 1984; McGrath et al., 1990).

3. Advancing technology.

I believe advances in technology to be one of the leading culprits in generating the increased rates of depression in Western-based cultures. Technology is a remarkable phenomenon. On the one hand, it permits extraordinary gains in some areas; on the other hand, these advances do not come without a high price in terms of our cultural psyche.

Technology has as its primary benefits speed and convenience. I remember a popular television commercial some years ago for an overnight mail company, which showed a busy executive speaking to many individuals on many telephone lines, all at high speed. The commercial's message was that in this fast world, the pinnacle of success was to be able to deliver mail overnight. The service was enthusiastically received, since mail normally took up to five days to get wherever it was going. Today, just a few years later, overnight mail has almost become obsolete because of the availability of fax machines, which can transmit documents and messages in seconds. Although these machines initially appeared in business offices, some Americans now feel they have to have one at home as well. And now that fax machines are an available option on new cars, we can be sure to have one when we're on the road—between work and home!

‣The emphasis on speed and convenience warps our perspective and places us at risk for emotional disturbances in ways with which we have yet to come to terms. The desire for speed and convenience is not unreasonable, of course, when one is considering doing something that can actually be done within such parameters, such as using a fax machine to send a letter. But what happens when someone applies these expectations of speed and convenience to a context wherein such criteria are entirely inappropriate, such as intimate relationships? Why do people expect to fall in love right away? Why do they strive for immediate intimacy by having sex on a first or second date? What is this trap that we have created for ourselves of expecting things—no matter how complex—to be achieved instantly? Our cultural emphasis on speed and convenience teaches us at all levels to develop a low tolerance for frustration. It results in individuals who can become anxious and depressed if they have to stand in line behind four other people at the bank. They feel victimized, isolated, and discounted simply because they have to wait a few minutes to make a deposit.

Clearly, our emphasis on speed and convenience relates to some of the most problematic patterns associated with depression, but I believe that the most significant technological advance in this regard is television. Research indicates that the average U. S. television set is on approximately 50 hours per week—an average of over seven hours per day (Sears, Peplau, Freedman, & Taylor, 1988)! The majority of American households also have cable television and video cassette recorders, and it is obvious to me that this immersion in television helps to shape individual and cultural perspectives more than does any other variable.

Among other things, television certainly reinforces the sensibility that demands and anticipates immediate gratification. We are continually shown that complex problems can be solved in an hour or so. Commercials promise to solve our problems within seconds. We are trained to expect quick resolution, even when it is unrealistic. Consider the recent Persian Gulf crisis. Active military intervention (aerial bombardment) took place over a span of roughly six weeks, and ground fighting for roughly 100 hours. In retrospect, that war is viewed as a very quick one. In thinking back, however, to the first air strike, I remember that the public was angrily demanding *immediate* news and *immediate* victory. People were complaining that "we are now into day 3 of the war." When the first week had passed, they were asking incredulously, both publicly and privately, "How can the war be going on so long?" Our cultural emphasis on speed sometimes supersedes our need to analyze the complexity of a given situation. It can lead people to do things brashly, underestimating what needs to be done. And, if success is not immediate, or failure is imminent, depression often follows.

The most troublesome aspect of television, however, is how it reinforces one of the most dysfunctional aspects of the typical depressed person's cognitive style, namely, global thinking (Beck, Rush, Shaw, & Emery, 1979; Blackburn & Davidson, 1990). Global thinking refers to the tendency to see the general picture, but not the component details; one sees the forest, but not the trees. Television *demands* global thinking. Actors play out intense and dramatic situations with little of the associated detail made evident to the viewer. For example, when a character is killed, the viewer doesn't see the related details, such as the making of funeral arrangements or the emotional effect on the family. The camera just moves to the next scene.

Global thinking is closely related to depression (Emery, 1988; Beck et al., 1979). It manifests as the depressed client just wanting to "be happy," to "be successful," or to "have a good relationship," but having no idea how to achieve these goals. Thus, television, fax machines, and home computers, and the social isolation, global thinking, and emphasis on speed and convenience that go with them, all help to create at a cultural level the mind set that can predispose people to depression.

4. The now orientation.

With technological advances and a corresponding deemphasis on tradition in our society, the direct suggestion is that *what matters the most is right now*, this moment. The outlook for our planet, our country, our families, and ourselves is bleak if we don't start to consider the longer-term consequences of our actions. By dissociating ourselves from eventual consequences, it becomes possible to engage impulsively in behaviors that will harm us later. How many clients became depressed through circumstances that could have been avoided with just a minimal amount of foresight?

It does not seem to be human nature, nor is it actively taught, to think beyond the moment (Ornstein & Ehrlich, 1989). The mental health profession, in this sense, has contributed to the problem with its overwhelming emphasis on the value of the person's "feelings in the moment." Clients are taught to recognize and respond to their feelings and to "live in the here and now." Such a philosophical orientation fuels impulsivity, a characteristic that already is too abundant. The impulsivity of our society permits the use of mind-altering drugs with little regard for the possibility of future addiction or dependence. Impulsive sexuality helps spread sexually transmitted diseases. Impulsive spending creates burdensome debts both for our government and for individuals who have charged to the limit on their credit cards. Perhaps the most unsettling example is found in the now orientation that is being applied at a planetary level. We recognize that rain forests, for example, are a primary source of our planet's oxygen, and that they are virtually irreplaceable, and yet we continue to cut them down at the rate of more than 50 acres a minute (*Time*, August 12, 1991).

Examples of the now orientation are virtually everywhere. As long as our society encourages such an orientation, we will continue to see individuals making decisions impulsively, with destructive consequences. For some, one of those consequences is depression.

There are far too many societal influences underlying depression than can be described here. It is necessary to appreciate that the depressed individuals you treat are, in part, products of society. Many of the most troublesome patterns that clinicians need to address are societally acquired, and so the skills one might wish to teach one's clients are not going to be reinforced in any place other than in the office. In a sense, the clinician needs to immunize the client against omnipresent destructive societal influences, teaching the client to identify and manage sources of threat (Koriath, 1989).

Familial Influences

The primary agents of socialization in a person's life are almost invariably his or her parents. The family is the context for many, if not all, of the major lessons in life: building relationships, developing communication skills, establishing life expectations, defining social roles, and delineating rules for living (i.e., what can be expressed, what cannot be expressed). A person's perceptions of reality are created largely through family interaction. From the standpoint of depression, familial influences on one's perceptions are especially significant.

I suggested earlier that depression is primarily a learned phenomenon, generated by how one organizes and then responds to the diverse experiences of life. Thus, it is not the events of one's life that cause depression, but the interpretation of and the significance attributed to those events; that is, the meaning that one makes of them. By examining more closely *how* someone makes meaning of experience, it may be possible to identify the specific mechanisms underlying that person's interpretations of "reality."

It has been established that the prevalence of depression is higher among first-degree biological relatives (American Psychiatric Association, 1987). The assumption has been that this is partial evidence in support of a genetic transmission factor (family histories and adoption studies provide further evidence). Although there may be some legitimate basis for accepting the notion of a genetic transmission factor, it is becoming increasingly clear that there is also likely to be a psychosocial transmission factor in effect (Arieti & Bemporad, 1978; Seligman, 1989). While growing up, a child observes, consciously and unconsciously, the explanations for life experiences of Mom, Dad, and significant others; the child then develops (through modeling) the same or similar patterns.

When considering the data regarding the presence of specific patterns typically associated with depression in both parent and child, the correlations are highly significant (Nolen-Hoeksema, Girgus, & Seligman, 1986; Katz & McGuffin, 1987; Bernstein, 1982). The child, in essence, learns the patterns for interpreting life modeled by the parents and significant others. These patterns may place the child at risk for depression—if and when circumstances arise later that highlight all that those patterns *prevent* the individual from doing effectively.

I want to emphasize that genetics and biochemistry can and do play an important role in depression. The research findings in support of this fact are quite substantial. For example, there are babies who, at birth, already manifest symptoms of depression (Trad, 1986; Arieti & Bemporad, 1978). But for the majority of individuals, it is the specific patterns learned (and *not* learned) through family socialization that predispose one to depression. Many of these specific patterns are described later in this book; others were described in *When Living Hurts* (1988).

Influences of Individual History

In moving from the cultural and familial to the individual influences on depression, one may come to realize that the specific patterns generated by one's unique personal history eventually serve as the risk factors for depression. The individual's idiosyncratic socialization history leads him or her to develop specific ideas, values, and ways of thinking and relating that collectively define that individual as unique. The specific kinds of experiences that one seeks out or is exposed to are generally a direct consequence of one's socialization. Therapy, ultimately, is aimed at this individual level, for it is the individual's specific patterns of thinking, feeling, behaving, relating, and perceiving that are the focal points of treatment. The therapist's task is to identify *how* this individual has learned to interpret and respond to life experience in ways that have placed him or her at a disadvantage, with depression as the outgrowth.

In this respect, it seems that depression is a predictable consequence of powerful experiences that the individual is not equipped to manage competently. Thus, as stated earlier, it is not so much what happens in a person's life that is the basis for depression; but *how* the person responds to the circumstances that determines whether depression will result, and, if so, how severe and chronic it is likely to be. Statistically speaking, most of us experience the same number of hurtful events. Virtually no one escapes rejection, disappointment, humiliation, abandonment, and other inherently painful experiences. Clearly, though, individuals vary in the way they perceive and respond to negative life experiences.

People can have horrendous personal histories that might seem to the casual observer reason enough for the onset of depression. The client whose mother died when he was young or the woman who was molested as a child—each has suffered an easily understood, easily recognized trauma that might explain the presence of depression later in life. However, such a simple cause-and-effect conclusion would be erroneous, as many people who have suffered similar traumas do *not* become depressed. Again, depression is not a product of the hurtful experiences themselves, but of some other, associated variables. I identify and describe these variables later in the book, with emphasis on their treatment with hypnotic approaches.

THERAPY FOR DEPRESSIONS

The need continually to evolve more effective treatments that focus on the most salient dimensions of depression is evident. What we have learned to date strongly suggests that much of what previously had been assumed about the treatment of depression is, in fact, not only irrelevant, but may be antitherapeutic (Yapko, 1988, 1989; Weissman, 1983). When we consider the many advances made in the psychotherapy of depression, there are substantial data to suggest that therapy needs to be *active* and *multidimensional*, emphasizing an educational and collaborative approach with the client. Cognitive therapy, and its associated models (cognitive-behavioral therapy, rational-emotive therapy, and so forth), have emerged as the psychotherapies of choice in treating depression (Becker & Heimberg, 1985; Seligman, 1989). Their emphasis is on bypassing poorly defined psychodynamic issues in favor of clarifying specific and definable errors in information processing that are consistently evident in the depressed client (Beck, 1976; Beck et al., 1979; Ellis, 1987).

Although I would not necessarily identify myself as a cognitive therapist exclusively, cognitive therapy methods are undoubtedly a powerful influence on my perspective. Their proved effectiveness and reliability unequivocally demonstrate the value of bypassing abstract issues in treatment in favor of building *concrete* and *specific* skills for thinking and for managing life competently. In this same type of framework, I will delineate patterns on many dimensions, including cognitive, that can be concretely defined and actively addressed through structured, experientially based therapy. The goal, of course, is to facilitate the client's recovery from depression at the earliest possible moment, while minimizing the possibility of later relapses.

There are at least two very compelling reasons why therapy for depression should be done in a brief therapy format that emphasizes active learning on the part of the client. First, depression has a high rate of spontaneous remission. In approximately 80 percent of individuals suffering major depression, the depression will spontaneously remit between four and ten months (APA, 1987). Thus, unless one operates in a brief therapy format (defined as ranging from one to 20 sessions), the client may be involved in a long-term therapy in which, after six or eight months, he or she shows a remission of symptoms. The clinician may interpret this as evidence of the effectiveness of the therapy, rather than consider the greater likelihood that the client just happened to be in treatment at the time of a spontaneous remission!

A second compelling reason why therapy is best done in a brief therapy context concerns the hazard that exists for the approximately 10 to 20 percent of these patients who become chronically depressed on the basis of what began as an acute episode (Davison & Neale, 1986; APA, 1987). In other words, 10–20 percent of depressed individuals suffering an acute depressive episode seemingly will make life decisions that maintain depression well past the point where it should have remitted. The sooner a clinician can actively intervene and prevent such a person from forming any inappropriate generalizations that might precipitate a chronically depressive outlook on life, the better. It is analogous to someone suffering the breakup of a romantic relationship and concluding, "I'll never fall in love again," and then never does. The depressed individual suffers some negative event and concludes, "I'll never be happy again," and then isn't. *The person's predictions about his or her own depression play an especially important role in treatment,* and so will constitute the subject matter of Chapter 7.

The above reasons for actively intervening in a brief therapy format are formidable. However, brief therapy can only be done when the most salient dimensions of depression are focused upon in a deliberate way. Focusing on nonsalient dimensions, like the hypothetical "anger-turned-inwards," is likely to lead to longer-term and probably ineffective therapy (Tavris, 1989). In this respect, I am especially mindful of the value of hypnosis in the treatment process. For the reader who has had formal training in hypnosis, many of the concepts and terms that I use in this book will be readily understandable and usable. But even the reader who is not well grounded in hypnotic concepts or methodologies can appreciate that *any* therapy focuses a person's attention on specific aspects of his or her experience.

Each clinician is faced with seemingly countless choices regarding the elements of experience to which he or she will direct a client's attention. For example, sending a client into a padded room to pound the walls in order to "get in touch with his anger" certainly amplifies in him an awareness of his angry feelings. However, the essential question becomes, "Is there a sound rationale and a therapeutic benefit in having him do so?" The data—and clinical experience—say "No" (Tavris, 1989; Murray, 1985). Sometimes the therapeutic folklore proves to be based on arbitrary beliefs rather than on real information, because, as it turns out, focusing depressed clients on their anger only makes them angry. It doesn't do much to alleviate depression (Tavris, 1989; Wender & Klein, 1981).

Hypnosis is a therapeutic tool for systematically amplifying dimensions of experience, and then associating those experiences to situations in ways that will be useful to the client. This book provides a framework for thinking about the experience of depression and for making use of current relevant learnings that can be taught in a variety of ways to the depressed client. Quite simply, the goal is to help him or her establish a different way of responding to life experience. As a therapeutic tool, hypnosis is multidimensional. It permits a clinician to amplify any dimension of experience (i.e., cognitive, behavioral, symbolic) that seems appropriate in the clinician's judgment. Furthermore, hypnosis is at the core of brief therapy approaches, including the ostensibly nonhypnotic but directive therapies. In this book, I describe how hypnosis came to be dissociated from the treatment of depression, and how shifts in one's viewpoint and techniques can make hypnosis an unusually valuable ally in the treatment process.

2

Depression and Hypnosis: Forbidden Friends

Few fields have been so beset by misconceptions as the field of clinical hypnosis. The primary reason for this is that hypnosis is so subjective an experience that it defies rigorous attempts at precise definition or measurement. In relation to depression, hypnosis has been so poorly understood and misapplied that it has come to be viewed as an incompatible modality of treatment. Just as in most aspects of psychotherapy, one's viewpoints about both hypnosis and depression dictate much of what becomes possible in treatment. In this chapter, I discuss the views of some of the leading experts in the field with regard to the use of hypnosis in treating depression, and describe a few hypnotic interventions that have managed to find their way into the literature.

MODELS OF HYPNOSIS

There are different models of hypnosis, just as there are different models of psychotherapy. Each model has its own underlying assumptions and associated techniques. In *Trancework: An Introduction to the Practice of Clinical Hypnosis* (Yapko, 1990), I detailed some of the differences among three general models: traditional, standardized, and utilization. The reader is encouraged to become familiar with these models, since they help define how one approaches treatment.

The emphasis in this volume is on utilization approaches to treatment, or what some call "Ericksonian hypnosis," for its originator, the late psychiatrist Milton H. Erickson, M.D. (Erickson & Rossi, 1979, 1981). It is important to establish the conceptual and practical differences among models of hypnosis, since it is the traditional model of hypnosis in particular that declares itself incompatible with the treatment of depressives. In essence, the traditional model views hypnosis primarily as an intrapersonal phenomenon, suggestibility as a stable trait of the individual, and suggestion as a direct communication requiring compliance (Weitzenhoffer, 1989; Spiegel & Spiegel, 1978). It is the model that has dominated the clinical literature since the days of Mesmer.

In contrast, the utilization approach views hypnosis as primarily an interpersonal phenomenon; suggestibility as variable, depending on personal, interpersonal, and contextual factors; and suggestion as varying from direct to indirect, depending on the client, and requiring collaboration (Zeig, 1980a; Gilligan, 1987).

The defining characteristic of utilization approaches is their naturalistic emphasis on accepting and utilizing the client's reality as the basis for the clinician's interventions (Erickson & Rossi, 1979, 1981). The utilization of the client's beliefs, values, strengths, weaknesses, personal history, and any other aspect of his or her subjective experience requires a client-centered approach that encourages meaningful collaboration and personal empowerment, not mere compliance. In the utilization model, hypnosis is done *with* the client, not *to* the client (Rossi, 1985; Gilligan, 1987). Further aspects of the utilization approach to hypnosis and psychotherapy are detailed in the next chapter.

EARLIER VIEWS ON HYPNOSIS AND DEPRESSION

It seems highly significant that in extensively researching the subject matter of this book, I found that most of the literature about the clinical applications of hypnosis did not offer even a single comment on its use in treating depressives, which in itself is a clear indication of how effectively hypnosis has been excluded from such treatment. Graham Burrows (1980) also conducted a comprehensive review of the literature on hypnosis and depression. He states:

From a review of the literature, it would appear that the use of hypnosis in the treatment of depression remains controversial . . . It would seem nevertheless that most experienced clinicians teach that severe depressive illness is a definite contraindication to hypnosis. Although they teach this, depressive illness appears to have received, for such an exceedingly common medical problem, minimal attention in most modern reference books on hypnosis. A possible interpretation is that the authors concerned may believe hypnosis has little place in the therapy of depression. (p. 167)

The fact that leading experts in the field of hypnosis have either totally ignored its potential applications in treating depression or have directly suggested that hypnosis is contraindicated leads one to ask, "What is it about hypnosis that is seemingly so hazardous in the psychotherapy of depressed clients that it is contraindicated as a treatment tool?" It is my contention that virtually every hazard associated with hypnosis, not only in the treatment of depression, but in the treatment of any disorder, is not a function of hypnosis itself, but of the manner in which it is applied.

Myths die hard and prejudices are difficult to overcome. This is as true in the field of clinical depression as it is in clinical hypnosis. The readily available data highlighting the consistently greater treatment success and demonstrably lower rates of relapse of cognitive and interpersonal therapies in the treatment of depression have not yet seemed to sway those therapists who assume minimally directive, psychodynamic, or issue-oriented perspectives of depression. Their viewpoint continues to be that brief therapy methods are somehow less intense, more superficial, and less comprehensive than a "deeper" therapy of a psychodynamic nature (Haley, 1987). It is difficult to accept viewpoints and methods that are not easily reconciled with one's preexisting framework.

The great majority of clinicians and authors discussing the subject of clinical hypnosis did not address the use of hypnosis in treating depression at all, thus indirectly stating their views that there is a fundamental incompatibility between hypnotic treatment and the problem of depression. Of the small number of authors who did discuss the use of hypnosis with depressives, most seemed to have the goal of so terrorizing their readers with anecdotes of (seemingly) hypnotically caused disasters that these readers would not dare to attempt to use hypnosis with their depressed clients. The hazards described most frequently fall into two basic categories: (1) the general inability of the depressed client to be hypnotized effectively or otherwise to benefit from hypnosis; and (2) the stripping away of the client's defenses, increasing his or her vulnerability to further psychic trauma, including the precipitation of psychosis or suicidal thoughts and feelings.

Many of the most highly regarded and experienced clinicians and authors in the field of clinical hypnosis have publicly taken a position that supports the presence of the so-called hazards of using hypnosis with depressives. Yet what clearly emerges from their collective perspective is simply a bias related to the many other established traditions of fear about and misunderstandings of hypnosis, perhaps starting most visibly with Sigmund Freud. Freud singlehandedly delayed progress in the field of hypnosis for decades—because of the erroneous views in which he had great confidence and his followers' blind faith in those views. Freud (1953) stated, "Hypnosis does not do away with resistance but only avoids it and therefore yields only incomplete information and transitory therapeutic success" (p. 269). However, as the clinical literature can easily attest (Erickson & Rossi, 1979; Haley, 1973, 1982; Spiegel & Spiegel, 1978), hypnosis is *not* just a symptomatic approach that yields transient results.

Doubts continue to linger about the true nature of hypnosis, as similar doubts linger about the nature of depression. The authors and clinicians who warned of the dangers of hypnosis for treating depression hold an outdated and fundamentally incomplete, sometimes even dangerous, representation of the phenomenon of depression in light of what we now know about who gets depressed and why. Attempting to treat depression when the fundamental conception of depression is unsound (such as its psychoanalytic conceptualization as necessarily rooted in anger, guilt, and loss) will predictably lead to an amplification of the nonsalient dimensions of the depressive experience, and perhaps even of its most negative and dangerous aspects. Thus, it is clear that the issue is *not* one of the viability of hypnosis for treating depression, but rather, of how it is applied.

What follows is a review of the literature on hypnosis, particularly as it relates to the view of hypnosis as a method of intervention contraindicated for depression.

THE "HAZARDS" OF HYPNOTIZING DEPRESSIVES

Inability to Be Hypnotized or to Benefit from Hypnosis

A significant number of practitioners have evolved the viewpoint that hypnosis is unlikely to benefit the client, either because the individual cannot be hypnotized, or because he or she is viewed as unlikely to benefit from hypnosis. Is the presumed inability to be hypnotized a product of the client's depression, a result of the client's responsiveness to the clinician and his or her methods, or are other factors involved? Consider the position taken by Herbert and David Spiegel (1978):

> This group [namely depressives], characterized by withdrawal and dysphoric affect, shows little willingness to *comply* [italics the author's] with any external signals. Reason becomes morbid rumination, with guilt and self-criticism the predominant theme. The feeling of sadness overwhelms all of their functioning and this affective state overshadows the actual reasons which exist in the world as a cause of sadness. The massive interference that a serious depression causes in an individual's intrapsychic and interpersonal functioning likewise seems to show itself in performance on the Hypnotic Induction Profile. (p. 140)

The reader will note the emphasis the Spiegels place on attaining compliance from the depressed client. Such an emphasis reflects a traditional orientation (in contrast to a utilization approach) in defining both the therapeutic and the hypnotic relationships. The demand for compliance inherent in the traditional approach lends itself to poor results with depressives in particular, whose motivation and ability to comply with seemingly arbitrary externals (like a command to perform an eye roll as part of the Spiegels' Hypnotic Induction Profile) are likely to be very low. It seems clear, then, that the Spiegels' finding a lack of responsiveness to their methods may be viewed more as a function of the way in which they define the therapeutic relationship than as a comment about the depressed individual's ability to respond meaningfully to hypnosis of a different methodology.

The Spiegels further cite a study by Silver (1973) that concluded that hypnotizability is consistent with one's general mental health. The Spiegels (1978) conclude: "This reflects our own findings that those who are significantly depressed are not hypnotizable" (p. 113). They go on to say, "Those with serious depressions may be so narcissistically withdrawn and devoid of energy that they cannot attend to the input signals" (pp. 148–149).

The Spiegels clearly recognize the marked internal absorption of the typical depressive client, and yet in attempting hypnotic therapy with such clients, they apparently ignore it as a basis for trance induction and employ methods that require compliance (i.e., an obedient responsiveness to externals). Such an approach is likely to fail because it does not fit into the frame of reference of the client, which is considered fundamental to the therapeutic hypnotic relationship (Gilligan, 1987; Yapko, 1990). This point is discussed in greater detail in the next chapter.

Another leading expert in hypnosis, Andre Weitzenhoffer, who is perhaps best known for his co-creation (along with Ernest Hilgard) of the Stanford Hypnotic Susceptibility Scales, also discourages the use of hypnosis with depressives. Weitzenhoffer (1989) states: "In general, I have not found hypnotism to be particularly useful with depressions" (p. 151). However, Weitzenhoffer does not seem to be as firm in his conviction, adding: "The reactive depressions (depressive neuroses) are one exception. Hypnotism with a supportive and re-educational approach can be quite effective in these cases."

But it is when depression is viewed in a psychoanalytic framework that the utilization of hypnosis in its treatment has been considered especially hazardous. For example, John Watkins (1987) states:

> One of the most frequent symptoms for which patients consult psychiatrists and psychologists is depression. Since this is commonly based in some underlying guilt or inhibited anger, direct suggestive therapy is seldom successful in achieving a permanent resolution. However, temporary elevations of good mood may serve to provide the necessary lift and revival of hope which can then be used to therapeutic advantage. (p. 69)

Burrows (1980) adds:

> The psychodynamics of depression often involve anger of an intense degree. In reactive depression, that which follows some disappointment in life, the anger may be easily traced to outer circumstances. In more complex cases, however, it may refer to a deeply repressed infantile anger going even as far as the oral stage of psychosexual development. The techniques of hypnosis move much more rapidly than ordinary psychotherapy into the situations involving "transference" distortions by the patient in which the therapist may be seen as an important figure from the past, often a parent or spouse. Such distortion may make the patient over-reactive to real or imagined slights from the therapist, or he may wish to "punish" the therapist for his imagined lack of care for the patient ... It is probably best to restrict the use of hypnosis for the mildly depressed, or moderately depressed person receiving antidepressants, and not to use this type of therapy in the severely depressed person. (pp. 168–169)

It is understandable why Watkins and Burrows would conclude that hypnosis is not desirable in the treatment of severely depressed patients when they view them from a psychoanalytic framework that emphasizes vagueries such as repressed anger. Unfortunately, this framework has little bearing on the etiology of depression. However, it does highlight that the way hypnosis is applied is invariably a function of how the clinician conceptualizes the nature of the problem and designs and delivers the associated therapeutic regimen. It has been a fundamental error in attempting to use hypnosis with depressed clients to approach them from a framework that amplifies the most destructive aspects of depressive phenomenology, such as anger or guilt, based on the arbitrary notion that these are at the root of depression.

Hypnosis Strips Defenses and Precipitates Unwanted Responses

The most common argument against the use of hypnosis in the treatment of depressed clients has been concern for an increased likelihood of suicide following hypnosis. It is as if hypnosis itself somehow strips the client of any reality orientation that would preclude making such a destructive and irrevocable choice. This view is destructive and misleading, and it needs to be dismantled once and for all. In days not long past, a similar myth existed in the depression literature that suggested that one should never ask a depressed individual whether he or she has suicidal thoughts or feelings. The fear was that merely mentioning it would suggest suicide to the depressed client (Nasr, 1982). We now know, of course, that this is ludicrous. Not only can suicide be discussed with depressed clients, but it is considered *necessary* to question the depressed client about any suicidal thoughts and feelings he or she may have so that one can assess the relative risks realistically (Beck et al., 1979; Klerman, Weissman, Rounsaville, & Chevron, 1984).

The hypnotic folklore might lead one to believe that not only is suicide a clear and ever-present danger in dealing with depressives, but that hypnosis, by definition, contains the potential to push the depressed client into suicide.

The Spiegels claim (1978) that the risk for suicide is, in part, a function of the client's unrealistic expectations for therapy:

> Some depressed patients may place unrealistic hopes in the trance experience as a way of ending their depression. Their magical wishes should be explored and defused before the induction is performed, to avoid having yet another hope dashed in a situation which could provoke a suicide attempt. (p. 19)

Given the Spiegels' emphasis on testing for suggestibility, which involves a pressure to perform and an implied ability to succeed or fail, it is more understandable why the depressed client could feel like a failure in this kind of hypnotic interaction. Their point that the client's expectations must be realistic is well considered. However, it is typically a core component of depression that a client's expectations are *not* realistic and are usually skewed in a negative direction (Beck, 1967). Rather than being an obstacle to treatment, hypnosis can be used to address that dysfunctional pattern (Yapko, 1988, 1989).

The danger of hypnosis precipitating suicide was also a concern for Harold Crasilneck and James Hall (1985). They state:

It is the risk of suicide, however, that makes depression dangerous, something to be treated carefully and with understanding.
The presence of frank suicidal thinking is a relative contraindication, in our opinion, to the use of hypnosis in an outpatient setting except in very special and rare circumstances . . .
Paradoxically, the most dangerous time in the treatment of
depression is when the patient seems to begin improving. Surprisingly, it is at this stage that suicide is most likely. Many have
speculated that the explanation for this chain of events is that
the severely depressed patient does not have the energy to consider suicide. As he or she begins to improve and energy levels
rise, action may become possible before the mood of depression
is thoroughly lifted. (pp. 322–323)

The quotation is a significant one in its illustration of fundamental
misconceptions about the nature of depression and suicide. To state
that the tendency to act on suicidal thoughts and feelings is a function of one's energy level, rather than of one's degree of hopelessness,
is indefensible (Beck, Steer, Kovacs, & Garrison, 1985; Beck, Brown,
Berchick, Stewart, & Steer, 1990). There are no data to suggest that
this is true. Contrary to the folklore, suicide is not a function of one's
energy; it is a function of one's expectations for the future. This topic
is addressed in detail in a later chapter because of its central importance in helping to establish a practical framework in which to conduct brief interventions with depressed clients.

Crasilneck (1980) later went on to elaborate on the same misconception when he said, "The danger period involving the severely
depressed patient is when you are 'teasing' them out of their depression, because they may attempt suicide at any time during that
period" (p. 115). This line of thinking would suggest that the client
is actually safer, though miserable, in the depths of depression.

The emphasis on hypnosis as a catalyst for suicide is evident in
still more of the traditional hypnosis literature. For example, Harold
Rosen (1981) describes the following:

A psychologist with pronounced sexual difficulties on a depressive basis requested hypnosis cure, but in view of his suicidal
depression was instead referred for psychiatric treatment. He

changed his mind, had another psychologist hypnotize him, and committed suicide. (p. 143)

Such anecdotes seem to suggest that the mere fact of being hypnotized was responsible for this psychologist's suicide, whereas we know nothing about the structure or the content of the hypnotic session(s) preceding the event. It is how and when the hypnosis was applied that matters, and this crucial information was omitted from the narrative as if it were irrelevant.

Ainslie Meares (1960), a well-respected contributor to the hypnosis literature, also condemned hypnotic treatment when he wrote:

The treatment of mental depression by hypnosis is much more complicated than might at first be expected. It is very common for patients to be referred in the belief that the feeling of depression can be dispelled by a few sessions of suggestive hypnosis. The danger of this approach is that the patient may commit suicide ... A trial of hypnotherapy usually leads to disappointment and may involve the patient in an unnecessary risk of suicide. (pp. 292–293)

Clearly, the way Meares conceptualizes depression is the underlying reason for his concern. His is the classic, but erroneous, view of depression as a consequence of unresolved feelings of loss.

[Depression] is essentially a pathological exaggeration of the normal psychological response to loss, particularly to loss of some affective relationship. Often the patient has an overwhelming sense of void. He is emotionally isolated. (p. 293)

Finally, two other experts lend support to the notion that hypnotic intervention is incompatible with depression. David Cheek and Leslie LeCron (1968) state flatly: "One of the contraindications for the non-psychiatrist in the use of hypnosis is to avoid it with anyone who is ... greatly depressed, suicidal ..." (p. 70). Why this statement was made is not elaborated, and so the reader is left to imagine the hazards they must have encountered that led to their conclusion.

The viewpoints of all the experts cited here, whose collective work for decades has guided the direction that the field of hypnosis has taken, seem to stem from the idea that depression is too dangerous a disorder (because of the potential for suicide) to treat hypnotically. Although some have conceded that hypnosis might be used in mild cases where suicide seemingly is not a present danger, in general the myth that hypnosis can precipitate suicide is starkly evident in their work. Their influence has, unfortunately, led most clinicians and authors to avoid considering how hypnosis might best be used for a depressed client's benefit.

Suicide aside, there are those who believe that hypnosis will aggravate the client's already delicate condition. Terman (1980) states:

> The risk of employing hypnosis to focus on the emotionally laden areas of a patient's life is that such an intense concentration might exacerbate the severity of the depression. (p. 201)

Miller (1979) adds to this concern the possibility of psychosis as a side effect of using hypnosis:

> States of agitation and communication blocks can often be markedly relieved and recollection enhanced. The resultant emotional catharsis may be quite beneficial to the patient; however, the therapist must be careful not to consciously confront such patients with traumatic and conflict laden revelations unless they are in such a state that they would be capable of handling these. Overloading the already damaged ego with additional emotional stress can precipitate serious psychotic reactions. (p. 185)

The Spiegels (1978) state:

> Depressed, especially endogenously depressed, patients with active suicidal ideation, should not be offered hypnotherapy as a first line of treatment. For some, hypnosis leads to temporary help, enough perhaps to facilitate acting out. (pp. 41–42)

Apparently, Terman, Miller, and the Spiegels share the notion that rather than enhancing the client's degree of control by focusing on useful dimensions of experience, the depressed client—through hypnosis—is invariably going to be drawn only to the destructive elements of experience, regardless of the influence of the clinician.

The client's death by suicide, psychotic reactions, and acting out are apparently not the only concerns in applying hypnosis. Milechnin (1967) states that simply the amplification of emotion in hypnosis can prove *fatal*:

> Even though no harm is done in the immense majority of cases, it is necessary to keep in mind that some exceptional case may appear, where the intensified disturbing emotion may exceed the limits of the person's tolerance . . . Is there any doubt that an intense emotional experience . . . may produce serious psychosomatic disorders? It is well-known that sudden death may result from emotions of this kind. (p. 195)

Apparently, not only should we not do hypnosis because of all the destructive potentials previously described, but we also should not encourage clients to express their strong feelings because of the fear of their sudden death from emotional overload! Such unfounded fears clearly indicate how much we as a profession still need to grow.

EARLIER HYPNOTIC STRATEGIES IN TREATING DEPRESSION

Although most traditional practitioners apparently consider hypnosis a poor choice for treating depressed individuals, some clinicians have described cases in which hypnosis was employed. In general, they have taken the position that when the threat of suicide is minimal or absent, or when the depression is clearly related to external circumstances (previously termed "reactive" depression), hypnosis is potentially useful.

Hypnosis may be used to suggest symptom removal and to address ongoing issues and patterns in the client's life. In this section, I describe some of the strategies and cases that have been described in the literature. It will again be apparent to the reader how each hypnotic intervention was employed within the clinician's preferred theoretical framework, which may have little, if any, bearing on the "real" reasons for the client's depression.

In addressing the issue of symptom removal, Terman (1980) states that "symptom amelioration alone (by hypnotic suggestion) is insufficient treatment if there is a major underlying psychodynamic conflict . . ." (p. 202). Crasilneck and Hall (1985) agree with Terman, stating:

When hypnotherapy is employed for treatment of a condition presenting primarily as depression, we are careful to avoid a symptom-removal approach. Suggestions are, "Your mind and your body will be free from tension, tightness, stress and strain . . . You will be able to cope with your problems more realistically . . . You'll be less tense and afraid." We do not give direct suggestions for the removal of the depression itself . . . (p. 323)

Though Crasilneck and Hall stated that they avoid a symptom removal approach, their direct suggestions are superficial and are clearly intended to remove symptoms. This incongruity represents one of the limitations of traditional hypnosis, a methodology in which one may tell a client what to do, and yet provide no means by which the client might be enabled to follow the suggestion. The fact that hypnosis, when employed, is so frequently aligned with a therapist's particular orientation strongly indicates the need to learn to adapt one's hypnotic techniques to the nature of the client's problem, rather than to some abstract theoretical formulations. For example, the following citations highlight the hazards of treating depression with hypnosis when one's understanding of hypnosis and depression are incomplete at best.

Lewis Wolberg (1948) states:

Hypnosis can aid some of the milder depressions. The trance state is used primarily as a means of inducing relaxation and as a vehicle for persuasion in the attempt to bolster self-esteem. A number of depressed patients appear to thrive under hypnotic therapy probably because it appeals to their dependency need. Mild depressions may be treated at home under supervision of a psychiatrically minded attendant or nurse, or, better still, the patient should be admitted to a rest home. Isolation from parents and friends, bed rest and constant care by a motherly attendant may prove very beneficial . . . Rest is important and a midday nap or rest period can be prescribed. Where it is essential for the depressed patient to continue work, dexedrine or benzedrine sulphate . . . may be helpful as a stimulant. Where these efforts fail to control the depression, electric shock therapy should be used. (p. 353)

Ainslie Meares (1960) elaborates on a similar theme:

In general, simple endogenous depression, agitated melancholia and the depressed phase of manic-depressive psychosis are not suitable for treatment by hypnosis. On the other hand, these conditions can be effectively treated by electro-convulsive therapy and the newer anti-depressant drugs. Difficulty arises when these conditions are present in only a mild degree. The patient and relatives are likely to be unwilling to undertake electro-convulsive treatment, and they may make strong demands for a trial of hypnosis. Such cases do not respond well to hypnosis. (pp. 292–293)

Meares goes on to describe a case involving a 35-year-old woman whom he describes as immature, and who became prone to psychosomatic symptoms and depression following her husband's death:

She made no improvement at all in eight sessions of hypnotic suggestion. On careful re-examination of the case, I realized that underneath her hysterical reactions there was in fact some real agitation. It now seemed that the patient had an early agitated melancholia with an overlay of hysterical features. She was given electro-convulsive treatment. There was immediate improvement, and she has remained well for the past two years. (p. 293)

A number of other cases have also been reported where hypnosis was used in the treatment of depressed individuals. Chambers (1968) reported on his successful use of hypnosis with a woman who resisted the use of antidepressant medications. He employed hypnosis (in ways not specified) to address her compulsion to eat raw potatoes, treating her within a psychodynamic framework. Rosen (1955) described the use of age regression with a suicidally depressed patient during which he helped the patient establish what he described as "more mature ego boundaries." Miller (1983) described a number of hypnotic techniques for treating depression, including modeling, cognitive restructuring, and reality testing. Gruber (1983) reported the use of hypnotherapy to teach the patient to respond to a spectrum of emotions, encouraging the patient to prevent himself from becoming immersed in a singularly depressed state of mind.

The use of physical and psychological relaxation techniques in the treatment of depression was described by Wright and Wright (1987), who framed the decision to participate in treatment on the part of the client as helping to establish an internal locus of control. They further described using hypnotic techniques involving fantasy, imagination, and age regression to amplify desired associations in the client. Perhaps the most unusual of the interventions described by the Wrights was the "suicide fantasy" conducted with a suicidal patient. With the guidance of a therapist, the client was encouraged to detail all aspects of his suicide imagery. The Wrights reported that doing so, and simultaneously expressing his associated feelings, helped free the patient from the pressure toward suicide, allowing him more easily to consider alternative life choices.

Edelstein (1981) described a severely suicidally depressed woman in her 40s with whom he conducted a hypnosis session. He induced trance, and established the ability to communicate with that "part" of her that caused her to remain so severely depressed. Edelstein simply suggested that that part, nicknamed the "Avenger" would leave. He reported that the patient let out a shriek "as though something had been pulled out of her" (p. 96), and that within days she no longer was depressed. Erickson (1980) reported on the case of a 25-year-old man who was depressed over an impending job loss. Erickson used hypnosis to facilitate a cognitive rehearsal of the relevant job skills. The client's performance improved so much that he did not lose his job, and his depression abated. Heller (1987) reported a case where he treated a depressed woman by using hypnosis to help her develop a visual imagery process by which she could visualize her feelings going from unpleasant to pleasant. Hodge (1990) described direct suggestions for the purpose of establishing a "time-out" period to delay the client's response to suicidal feelings. He offered suggestions such as the following:

The more suicidal you are, the more you will be compelled to enter trance and contact me. In the trance, you will be unable to commit suicide unless I give you permission. The trance itself may be just the factor you need to break up your suicidal thoughts and to help you to relax and find better ways to handle your problems. (p. 332)

Havens and Walters (1989) offered a number of hypnotherapy scripts to be used verbatim with depressed clients, based on the belief that depression is related to feelings of helplessness and worthlessness. In one script, entitled "The Wreck," they employed a metaphor intended to address a dynamic of underlying anger. In a second script, entitled "Royal Service," the authors offered a scripted metaphor about depression resulting from a desire to please or protect others. They further offered a direct hypnotic suggestion script in which the symptoms of depression are simply suggested away so the client may find the motivation to orient to positive experiences of life.

The views presented in this chapter that espouse a negative view of hypnosis relative to depression highlight what can happen when the broad set of patterns available in the field are applied narrowly from within a particular viewpoint. Likewise, the examples offered by those who have used hypnosis in treatment successfully highlight what happens when the same sort of patterns are applied more broadly with flexibility and creativity, and with an emphasis on the unique characteristics of each particular client.

Considering the various perspectives and approaches described in this section, it is clear that ultimately it is how hypnosis is applied that determines its viability as a treatment tool. And how it is applied is a direct consequence of how both depression and hypnosis are conceptualized.

GOING BEYOND WHAT HAS BEEN

The point has been made that hypnosis generally either has been ignored or has been viewed as contrary to the treatment of depressed individuals. These views are outdated for two reasons: (1) our understanding of depression has changed, and (2) our understanding of hypnosis has changed.

Depression is not the mystery it once was. Moving beyond older psychodynamic, and now untenable, views of depression as purely a product of loss or anger turned inward, we are now in a better position to focus on very specific patterns an individual employs in organizing his or her subjective experience as the appropriate target(s) for treatment. Thus, the use of hypnosis exclusively to amplify feelings of anger, to bring out feelings of loss, to relive painful traumas, or to "heal the inner child," can reasonably be expected to be unsuccessful. Demanding compliance, immersing the person in his or her descriptions of subjective pain, and other such techniques that amplify destructive and less potentially therapeutic aspects of depression can now be viewed as contraindicated approaches.

The traditional approach to hypnosis that is characterized primarily by direct suggestions offered in an authoritarian style, aimed either at symptom removal or at resolution of (hypothetical) psychodynamics, is not now and has never been a singularly viable treatment approach. Furthermore, in recent years the realization has evolved that it is not merely the presence or absence of some state ambiguously called "trance" that is the mechanism of healing, but rather it is the way in which the clinician elicits and guides the inner associations of the client's world (Erickson & Rossi, 1979; Erickson, Rossi, & Rossi, 1976). Thus, when *any* clinician reports favorably or unfavorably on the use of hypnosis in the treatment of a specific client or client population, he or she is reporting on the effectiveness of his or her methods in response to a particular client. It is an overgeneralization to assume that it is a statement regarding the viability of hypnosis as a treatment with clients similarly diagnosed.

This perspective reflects a recent evolution in the thinking of mental health professionals in general. Previously, the tendency has been to bypass any examination of clinical technique, and of the clinical rationale underlying the technique, while assuming that it is the client who bears full (or most) responsibility for a successful treatment. If the client did not improve, it was because of his or her resistance— that is, a lack of will to change—or it was due to secondary gains from the symptoms, or to other factors that blocked the clinician's efforts to help. This attitude is also pervasive in the hypnosis literature. There is an attitude that encourages "blaming the victim" when a depressed client does not respond to the clinician's hypnotic suggestions or treatment plan. Consider, for example, this statement by Meares (1960), which is typical of that orientation:

> In hypnotizing patients who suffer from a reactive depressive state, it is well to remember that the patient needs and yearns for a further emotional relationship. This facilitates the formation of rapport and the induction of hypnosis. At the same time, the depressed patient is at first inclined to reject offers of emotional support, *he wants to feel his loss* [italics the author's]. The idea of a new emotional relationship somehow seems to conflict with his feeling of loyalty to the person whom he has lost. The result is that these forces tend to hold the depressed patient back when the therapist moves to establish rapport. Accordingly, it is necessary to proceed slowly both in the preliminaries to hypnosis and in the induction itself. (pp. 293–294)

Though stated somewhat differently, Havens and Walters (1989) reveal a similar perception that depressed clients are motivated to stay depressed.

> Many depressed clients are reluctant to change their way of thinking. They seem to cling to their misery, either because they believe it is their right to feel awful given what life has done to them, or because they feel that somehow it would be wrong to feel better. (p. 84)

This attitude of blaming the client when therapy does not proceed as the clinician wishes is a pattern ripe for change. In light of what we now better understand about how people structure their subjective experience, it is becoming increasingly clear that, in most cases, the client's response to treatment—including hypnosis—is a function of some very specific identifiable factors. Addressing these factors carefully will yield a corresponding increase in positive responses to treatment. Some of the key factors in utilizing hypnosis skillfully in the treatment of depressed clients are described in the next chapter.

3

Hypnosis: Is It What You Think It Is?

Contrary to popular misconception, hypnosis is *not* a specific methodology that all practitioners apply similarly. The methods of hypnosis delineated throughout this volume of necessity will be conceived subjectively and practiced idiosyncratically by the reader who chooses to employ them. It is analogous to learning a common language, which each person will then speak in his or her own way. In promoting hypnosis as a therapeutic tool for treating depression, I encourage the recognition that patterns of influential communication are the essence of effective psychotherapy, and that these patterns can be learned and applied systematically to the great benefit of depressed clients (Yapko, 1988, 1989).

DEFINING HYPNOSIS

No precise definitions for subjective experiences exist. In the same way that one would have difficulty offering a standard definition for such experiences as love, anger, curiosity, and spiritual connectedness, one would be hard pressed to offer a definition of hypnosis. Hypnosis has not yet been defined in more than imprecise phenomenological terms, and frankly, I do not believe that it will be, simply because of its inherently subjective nature.

With this in mind, I will attempt to offer a definition that at least describes some of the principal elements of the applications of clinical hypnosis in the context of psychotherapy. This definition applies only to the *practice* of clinical hypnosis, whereas descriptions offered later in this chapter attempt to describe the *experience* of hypnosis from the client's standpoint. Thus, I offer this as a guiding definition: hypnosis is a process of influential communication in which the clinician elicits and guides the inner associations of the client in order to establish or strengthen therapeutic associations in the context of a collaborative and mutually responsive goal-oriented relationship (Rossi, 1986; Erickson & Rossi, 1979; Yapko, 1990).

In the above definition, there are certain key aspects of the therapeutic relationship worthy of elaboration. In describing hypnosis as a process of influential communication, I am suggesting that interpersonal influence is a mechanism of altering the experience of others. The ability to influence another is inherent in any interpersonal context. The evidence for this point is quite simple: You will do things by yourself that you will not do if another person is present. *The mere presence of someone else changes what you do* to some extent. How one may use patterns of influence deliberately and skillfully is the artistry of hypnosis, and this requires an in-depth understanding of patterns of communication, information processing, relationship dynamics, personality variables, and numerous other relevant factors (Sherman, 1988).

In suggesting that the role of the clinician is to elicit and guide the inner associations of the client, I am stating that hypnosis in and of itself is not inherently therapeutic. *Anything that has the potential to be therapeutic, has an equal potential to be antitherapeutic;* a clinician unwittingly can establish, despite the most benevolent of intentions, associations that are harmful for the client. Hypnosis is a process wherein one's communications are used to generate meaningful experience within the client. Therefore, it is important that hypnosis be used to elicit and guide associations that will prove beneficial, yet it is the idiosyncratic inner world of the client—his or her inner associations—that dictates that individual's responses. It is well recognized that we all respond to our own subjective frames of reference (i.e., internal associations, viewpoints, interpretations, and perceptions) in responding to life experience. Hypnosis is used to identify and alter these inner associations of the client's subjective world view (Zeig, 1980a).

The definition of hypnosis provided also includes the notion of a collaborative and mutually responsive goal-oriented relationship. Previously, hypnosis was employed in an attempt to impose desirable beliefs or associations on the client through direct suggestion, thus requiring a high level of compliance on the part of the client. Hypnosis, in order to be effective with the widest range of clients possible, must involve a collaborative, positive working relationship between clinician and client. "Rapport" has always been emphasized as important, but having rapport is not the same thing as defining the relationship as collaborative. The clinician may know things that the client does not know that would be of benefit, but such information is virtually useless if the client is not in a position to understand and make effective use of what the clinician knows. Thus, to succeed, the clinician is required to adapt his or her communications to the client's style of thinking and relating. The clinician must respond to the client's concern, as well as individual style, and as the clinician adjusts his or her demeanor and style of intervention to the client's needs or abilities, the client can be more responsive to the clinician's guidance (Zeig, 1987; Erickson, Rossi, & Rossi, 1976). This interaction constitutes a circular process of continuous feedback and adaptation between clinician and client.

Given the emphasis on these relational aspects of hypnosis as a therapeutic tool, it is easy to discover how the characteristics of hypnosis can be seen in virtually any therapy; every psychotherapy includes a large element of suggestion. After all, there is the inherent suggestion to the client in any therapeutic intervention that says, in essence, "You'll get better if you do this." The hypnotic aspects of psychotherapy are elaborated in greater detail in the next chapter.

It is important to reiterate the point that because the elements of suggestion are inherently present in any therapy, if the treatment places too great an emphasis on nonsalient—or even destructive—aspects of the client's experience, the outcome is likely to be less than beneficial, or even antitherapeutic. It is clear that those clinicians who hold the perception that hypnosis is contraindicated in the treatment of depression could only have reached such a conclusion through a misguided application of hypnosis.

Any clinician dealing with a suicidal individual, for example, must *say* something and *do* something to influence this individual for the better. Whatever one says or does in therapeutically influencing such a fragile individual would be defined as hypnotic, given the relatively broad definition of hypnosis just outlined. According to this expansive use of the term "hypnosis," which includes patterns of influential communication *even in the absence of a formal trance induction,* one is altering the client's subjective experience and focusing him or her on inner associations. *Patterns of hypnosis can be used anywhere that focused therapeutic influence is desirable.*

I encourage a broad and flexible conception and practice of hypnosis. I reject out of hand the past assumptions about hypnosis as contraindicated for depressives as either erroneous or irrelevant to the modern clinical practice of hypnosis and psychotherapy. However, by expanding the parameters of what may be defined as hypnotic, I am deemphasizing some of the rigid and arbitrary criteria that have previously limited the applicability of hypnosis in treatment, and not just of depressives, but of other client groups as well. The following list delineates some of the fundamental assumptions that succinctly represent the conceptual and philosophical framework for the utilization approaches to treatment described in this book and the companion volume, *When Living Hurts*.

TABLE 1. ASSUMPTIONS REGARDING DIRECTIVE APPROACHES

- Influence is inevitable.
- Communication is the vehicle of the therapy.
- Therapy is goal directed and facilitated by the clinician.
- The client is operating on the basis of subjective interpretations of reality, which, in depressed individuals, are generally erroneous and/or depressogenic.
- The client is not "sick," but is symptomatic on the basis of inadequate skills, problem-solving methods, and a limited range of responses in a given context.
- The clinician accepts and utilizes the client's frame of reference.
- Rapport is a key to successful influence.
- The client's relationship to the clinician is integral to the therapy.
- Directives make use of contextual variables.
- Symptomatic patterns coexist on multiple levels.
- Insight is not necessary for change to occur, and may even be antitherapeutic.
- Directive approaches make use of client resources.
- Resistance may be intrapersonal and/or interpersonal.
- Directives facilitate the integration of positive learnings.

These assumptions may seem self-explanatory, but directly and indirectly, they help form the foundation for much of the discussion throughout this book.

WHY USE HYPNOSIS IN TREATMENT?

In previous writings (Yapko, 1990), I have made a distinction between what I have termed "formal" and "informal" hypnosis. By formal hypnosis, I mean hypnotic procedures that are overtly identified as such: "Now we're going to do hypnosis. Sit comfortably . . . Close your eyes." By informal hypnosis, I mean the use of deliberate strategies to focus the client and guide his or her inner associations for the purpose of establishing a therapeutic shift in the person's subjective experience. Thus, hypnosis is a flexible and goal-oriented tool to be used in the context of a therapeutic relationship.

Though most therapists readily recognize the uniqueness of each individual conceptually, they begin to treat people with similar presenting problems as if they were all more or less the same. The utilization approach to hypnosis demands continuous adaptation to the unique subjective reality of each individual client. Thus, the client's views of reality are utilized (hence, the name "utilization" approach) in the service of the therapeutic goals (Erickson & Rossi, 1979, 1981; Zeig, 1980a; Erickson, Rossi, & Rossi, 1976). Furthermore, immersion in the hypnotic framework permits the insight that the meaning of experience is determined in large part by the context in which it takes place (Watzlawick, Weakland, & Fisch, 1974).

There are few, if any, absolutes of experience or individual patterns that are unilaterally good or bad; there are only context-bound definitions of what is or is not useful. Rationality is neither a good thing nor a bad thing; its value depends on when and how it is applied. Hypnosis is not a good thing or a bad thing; its worth is derived from the consequences of when and how it is applied. Assertiveness is not a good thing or a bad thing; it can generate either helpful or harmful results, depending on when and how it is applied. Thus, the use of hypnosis presupposes a framework in which it is recognized and accepted that interpretations of "reality" are subjective, and that it is one's subjective frame of reference that dictates one's responses to the ongoing stimuli of life experience (Watzlawick, 1984; Hoffman, 1990).

There are some outstanding reasons to use hypnosis in the context of psychotherapy in general, and with depressives in particular: (1) it amplifies portions of subjective experience, making it easier to recognize where the client's patterns of perception, thinking, relating, and so forth, are causing or maintaining his or her experience of depression; (2) it serves as a potent method of therapeutic pattern interruption; (3) it facilitates experiential learning; (4) its use helps associate and contextualize desired responses; (5) it models flexibility, encouraging a variety of ways to relate to one's self; and (6) it helps to build focus. Each of these advantages is discussed in detail in the following sections.

AMPLIFYING SUBJECTIVE EXPERIENCE

A core task of hypnosis in particular—and psychotherapy in general—is to amplify aspects of experience in the client's awareness and associate them to some meaningful context. Thus, our understanding of which aspects of experience to amplify becomes a critical component of therapy, one that will predict the likelihood of therapeutic success. Experience can be thought of as occurring across many dimensions simultaneously. These dimensions include, but are not limited to, the physiological, affective, behavioral, contextual, relational, symbolic, historical, and cognitive (Zeig, 1980b; Yapko, 1988).

Each of these dimensions plays an important role in the quality of ongoing experience. Furthermore, each therapeutic modality emphasizes the prominence of experience in a particular dimension—cognitive therapy focuses primarily on the cognitive dimension of experience, interpersonal therapy focuses on the relational dimension, behavioral therapy focuses primarily on the behavioral dimension, medical interventions focus on the physiological dimension, psychodynamic therapy focuses on the symbolic and historical dimensions, and so forth. It is debatable whether, in a given client's case, that particular dimension of experience is actually the best target for the intervention. Often, what delays or prevents therapy from succeeding, or what generates undesirable results, is the inappropriate amplification of a nonsalient, or even potentially harmful, aspect of experience. For example, although, as described in the previous chapter, Wright and Wright (1987) reported a successful therapeutic outcome in the case of a suicidal individual who was encouraged hypnotically to carry out the suicide, I would speculate that most clinicians would agree that this is a very risky maneuver and appropriate in only the most extreme circumstances. It has the potential to desensitize the individual to thoughts and images of suicide; furthermore, some clients might be inclined to act out their suicidal feelings if no additional intervention is used to curtail the client's sense of hopelessness. In this respect, the point is once again highlighted that it is not hypnosis per se that helps or hurts the (depressed) client, but it is how the hypnosis is utilized. The chief function of hypnosis is to amplify specific portions of subjective experience in order to make them more readily accessible in treatment. Thus, hypnosis may, in a broad sense, be used either diagnostically or therapeutically.

From a diagnostic standpoint, hypnosis may be used as a technique of "uncovering" in order to identify underlying issues (if one is psychodynamically oriented) (Brown & Fromm, 1986) or, as is advocated in this book, to identify ongoing depressogenic patterns. The identification of patterns that cause and maintain the individual's depression is obviously a necessary precursor to interrupting those patterns therapeutically and establishing more adaptive ones.

Hypnosis may be used therapeutically to structure new experiences that may establish new associations in the client. It affords one a multidimensional perspective as well as a multidimensional treatment regimen. Rather than focusing exclusively on physiology, on relationships, on cognition, on history, or on any singular dimension of experience, hypnosis may be used to amplify any and all of them.

HYPNOSIS AND PATTERN INTERRUPTION

The guiding definition of psychotherapy throughout this volume (and the companion volume, *When Living Hurts*) is "pattern interruption and pattern building." There are literally hundreds of psychotherapies, all of which differ quite markedly in terms of content: One focuses on thoughts, and another on feelings. One focuses on intrapsychic dynamics, whereas another focuses on interpersonal relationships. The possible variations in content are limitless. However, at the structural level, all therapies seem to have as a common denominator the tasks of interrupting ongoing patterns of client experience and of building new, more adaptive patterns. Hypnosis is a powerful tool for both aspects of the therapy process.

Consider the client seeking treatment who is experiencing negative ruminations, agitation, anxiety, and other common symptoms of depression. The individual is exposed to a rudimentary hypnotic induction in which only a superficial experience of relaxation is facilitated. An intervention as simple and superficial as a relaxation procedure can still have dramatic therapeutic results. Some of those who have encouraged the use of hypnosis in the treatment of depressives have noted the benefits of hypnotic relaxation (Hammond, 1990; Terman, 1980). But although hypnosis for the mere purpose of relaxation is probably its least significant application, it is still potentially of therapeutic value simply because it interrupts the client's ongoing symptomatic experience. The depressed client who experiences even a brief period of relief from agitation, anxiety, negative ruminations, and other such troublesome and immediate symptoms is taking a very important step toward establishing the recognition that *subjective experience is malleable, not fixed.* Thus, even a less-than-skilled clinician applying methods of hypnotic relaxation can generate some useful therapeutic responses, if only because of the pattern-interrupting capabilities of hypnotic induction and relaxation.

HYPNOSIS AND EXPERIENTIAL LEARNING

Beyond question, the most valuable form of learning is experiential learning when trying to teach the life skills (i.e., pattern building) that can minimize episodes of depression. In this respect, hypnosis is of enormous value in its emphasis on direct experience. It can be used to facilitate insight, or it may be used to facilitate changes in perceptual, behavioral, or other responses in the absence of insight. But however one uses hypnosis, the primary emphasis is on experiential learning—learning through direct experience rather than through modeling or other less direct methods. This is not to say that such modeling strategies are not employed, but rather that the emphasis is placed on the client's absorption in the associations that are elicited and guided through the clinician's interventions.

Trance experience is not rational. There is a recognition among practitioners of hypnosis that, in general, the most meaningful trances absorb the client in structured but arbitrary experiences that would not be possible in terms of "objective" reality (Erickson, Rossi, & Rossi, 1976; Zeig, 1980a). For example, in order to facilitate the resolution of a client's unresolved feelings toward a deceased parent, hypnosis may be used to have the client hallucinate an interaction with the parent in which communication for the purpose of achieving closure is possible. The client may then have the subjective experience of having said what needed to be said, even though, by objective standards, the interaction was not possible. A great benefit of the skillful application of hypnosis is that the clinician no longer is bound by the rigid parameters of so-called "reality." Thus, a depressed client can directly experience successful interactions—achieving closure on unresolved issues, asserting control rather than being a victim, or countless other experiential learnings—which can be applied later in other relevant contexts.

Experiential learning is of particular importance among depressives. Research indicates that depressives tend toward concrete thinking in terms of their cognitive style (Beck et al., 1979; Burns, 1980). This suggests, in part, that unless a client directly *experiences* a relevant learning and is then methodically instructed as to when and where it applies, it is unlikely that the client will make the best use of that learning. This is one of the main reasons why many psychotherapists who work with depressed clients often feel frustrated by their seemingly slow progress in treatment. However, when therapeutic learnings are structured in a way that takes into account the cognitive style of the depressed client, the rate of progress increases proportionately. Experiential learning plays the key role in the successful treatment of depression.

Hypnosis Associates and Contextualizes Desired Responses

Among the frustrations that clinicians include when describing feelings of burnout in working with depressed clients is how frequently important ideas seem to need to be repeated. One of the main components of any successful psychotherapy, and of psychotherapy with depressed individuals in particular, is the need to contextualize learnings. In other words, one may have the therapeutic goal of clarifying an important point about exhibiting some desirable behavior or developing a more rational way of thinking, but, if the teaching is not concretely defined and deliberately linked to a specific context within the depressed client's world, the teaching is not likely to be integrated.

"Contextualization" refers to the process of associating a desired response with a specific situation (Gilligan, 1988). In the realm of hypnosis, this is the job of the "posthypnotic suggestion," a suggestion given to the individual during hypnosis about some response he or she is to generate in some later context, ostensibly after the trance state has been terminated (Hilgard, 1968; Kroger, 1977; Erickson & Rossi, 1979; Erickson, 1958). Without the use of post-hypnotic suggestions to serve as a bridge between the hypnotic state and the person's "usual" waking state, it is highly probable that whatever gains might have been made during the hypnosis session will be limited to that session and not extended to the rest of the client's life.

Contextualization is necessary if any integration of therapeutic learnings is to take place. When a client seems to understand at an intellectual level what the clinician is teaching but does not apply it, this should serve as a strong cue to the clinician to pay more attention to issues of contextualization. A chief function of hypnosis as a tool for eliciting and guiding associations of the client is to assist the individual in recognizing *specific* opportunities to implement relevant learnings. The use of hypnosis to offer practice opportunities (what some might call a "cognitive rehearsal") is just one way to accomplish this (Beck et al., 1979).

MODELING FLEXIBILITY

Besides its value for contextualizing experiential learnings, there are other reasons to employ hypnosis in treating depressives. Just the use of hypnosis models a behavioral and relational flexibility. Hypnosis encourages experimentation as a way of intervening. When it is introduced into the therapeutic relationship, it communicates to the client—directly and indirectly—a shared purpose: "We can relate to each other in a variety of ways. There is no rigid formula for what we must do here. We can be mutually responsive, and in a collaborative way we can experiment with going beyond the boundaries of perception that have been established by you to your own detriment." Furthermore, the use of hypnosis not only encourages a systemic viewpoint, but it demands one because, by definition, its use acknowledges depression as a multidimensional experience. The client comes to understand that depression is not the result of a single problem, that there is not a direct cause-and-effect relationship between one particular issue and depression. And to introduce marital therapy or family therapy into the treatment, if indicated, becomes easier when the relationship between the client and the therapist is multifaceted and flexible. Hypnosis facilitates a broader, multidimensional outlook.

BUILDING FOCUS

Still another reason to make use of hypnosis in treatment is the role it can play in building a client's focus. Certain disorders are characterized, in part, by an impairment of attentional focus. Extreme anxiety, physical pain, and depression are all disorders that, by their very nature, impair the client's ability to focus meaningfully (Cleve, 1985; Emery, 1988). It is on this basis that some clinicians have concluded that depressed individuals cannot be meaningfully engaged in hypnotic interaction. To expect someone who is intensely absorbed in uncomfortable, even painful, internal experience to comply with arbitrary external demands (e.g., an eye roll or an arm levitation) is simply too much to expect. However, it is clear if the client is to benefit not only from hypnosis, but from therapy, he or she will need to develop enough focus to participate in a significant way. Hypnosis as a focusing technique can assist in this process.

It is interesting how the interpretation of (ambiguous) client responses dictates a clinician's reactions. The impairment of attentional style associated with depression is usually obvious: You conduct a therapy session with your depressed client in which you (naturally) offer penetrating insights and valuable recommendations, and you enthusiastically encourage your client to give a great deal of consideration to the content of the session in order to be able to discuss it further next time. The client returns a week later, and you ask, "Did you give much thought to what we spoke about last week?" The client looks puzzled and slightly vacant, and responds with a question, "Did I see you last week?" Historically, therapists have interpreted such lack of consideration or application of important ideas as the "resistance" of the depressed client. Many assume a motivation to maintain depressive symptoms. Such a "blame-the-victim" perspective precludes establishing a progressive therapeutic relationship.

If the clinician does not recognize that depression impairs the client's ability to focus—and that a concrete cognitive style generally precludes carrying over information from one context to another (without guidance), and that trance responses are trance-state specific (i.e., tied to the state of hypnosis)—then the clinician might naturally interpret the client's lack of use of skills or ideas provided in therapy as evidence of resistance. Thus, it is my recommendation that before any major therapeutic interventions are attempted, the clinician assess the quality of the client's attentional style. If the client's attention span is marginal because of the depression, then the clinician might spend a couple of sessions providing some general relaxation and focusing techniques to help build an attention span adequate to utilize in therapy. *It is highly recommended that such hypnotic processes be tape recorded and the tapes given to the client.* Repeated practice can help establish an increasing ability to focus meaningfully.

CONTRAINDICATIONS

I have outlined some of the essential contributions that hypnosis makes to effective psychotherapy with depressed clients. However, the question is commonly posed to me: "What are the contraindications for the use of hypnosis?" Given my definition of hypnosis as influential communication in which the client's experience is meaningfully guided in a therapeutic direction, my answer is unequivocal: I know of no context in which skillful communications are contraindicated. It bears repeating that problems are virtually never caused by hypnosis itself; however, they can arise when hypnosis is misapplied and the client is unintentionally directed to associate to experiences that are antitherapeutic.

This view of hypnosis has not been adequately elaborated upon in the literature. Thus, there are a number of common misconceptions among clinicians who are either completely unfamiliar with hypnosis, or who are only familiar with the outdated practice of hypnosis as an exclusively direct and authoritarian approach that aims at resolution of hypothetical psychodynamic issues or mere symptom amelioration. In the next section, these misconceptions are identified and briefly addressed.

MISCONCEPTIONS ABOUT THE USE OF HYPNOSIS IN TREATING DEPRESSION

Misconceptions about hypnosis are pervasive both in the mental health profession and among the general public. Whenever a clinician applies hypnosis, the results are invariably a product of what was done, how it was done, why it was done, when it was done, to whom it was done, and the context in which it was done. Hypnosis is a tool. Neither good nor bad, it is simply a way of communicating ideas in the context of a relationship. The artistry of using hypnosis skillfully as an effective tool in treating depression is in recognizing and utilizing the many variables that will influence the client's ability to acquire the relevant experiences and learnings in order to recover.

In this section, I describe some of the most common misconceptions about hypnosis relevant to the treatment of depressed clients. I address each briefly, with the goal of encouraging confidence on the part of the reader to use hypnosis sensitively for therapeutic purposes.

Hypnosis Is a Therapy

Hypnosis is *not* a therapy; it is a therapeutic tool. It is a vehicle for expressing ideas and making contact with different aspects of the client's ongoing experience. Various people may say that they use hypnosis, but that suggests nothing about the similarities among their methods and styles. Hypnosis, in the utilization framework, is a vehicle of influential communication—a definition that refers only to its structure, not to its content. Thus, hypnosis may be employed in communicating ideas commonly related to cognitive therapy, or it may be used to communicate ideas commonly related to interpersonal psychotherapy or to communicate ideas from *any* form of therapy. In other words, when employing hypnosis with a particular client, the fact that hypnosis is used does not indicate whether the intervention is aimed at a cognitive, a behavioral, a physiological, or some other dimension of the client's experience. This is why hypnosis is so compatible with virtually any approach to therapy. Hypnosis simply amplifies whatever it is about that therapy that makes it therapeutic, but it is not an independent form of therapy.

Hypnosis Involves a Loss of Control

I have never had a client present to me a desire to lose control of himself or herself. In fact, it's quite the opposite: clients routinely ask to enhance their sense of control over their life experiences.

One of the most significant therapeutic aspects of hypnosis is its ability to increase the client's sense of control. One can easily imagine what it does for a client's self-image to discover that he or she can control his or her level of anxiety or his or her responses to a particular individual or situation. The value of hypnosis lies in its ability to establish access to resources otherwise seemingly outside one's range of abilities.

The image of hypnosis as some sort of mechanism for losing control is propagated most obviously by the media (movies, television shows) and entertainers (stage hypnotists). More subtle, but just as likely to perpetuate misguided ideas about hypnosis, are those clinicians who employ hypnosis from an exclusively authoritarian position in which suggestions are imposed on the client, whose role is relegated to one of mere compliance if he or she is to be deemed successful. Such clinicians assert power over the client and thereby define the relationship as one in which the client is "one down." Such an approach unwittingly reinforces one of the most troublesome patterns associated with depression; namely, that too often the client is already likely to define himself or herself as one down relative to others. It is fundamental in a therapeutic relationship that the relationship between clinician and client be a collaborative and mutually responsive one (Beck et al., 1979, 1987; Gilligan, 1987). Of the various models of hypnosis, it is only the utilization approach to hypnosis described herein that emphasizes this concept. Thus, earlier considerations of hypnosis in relation to depression were probably quite accurate in the observation that depressives did not respond well to hypnotic treatment. The error was in taking this as a statement about the response of depression to hypnotic treatment instead of as a statement about the hypnotist's approach.

Hypnosis Encourages Dependency

This misconception about hypnosis is particularly relevant in treating depression. This volume specifically addresses the diagnostic category known as major depression, but it is common among individuals suffering from major depression also to manifest associated personality disorders, the most prevalent of which is the dependent personality disorder (Kocsis & Frances, 1988; Charney, Nelson, & Quinlan, 1981). In any therapy, but especially in cases of comorbid disorders, dependency is a significant factor to consider in the therapy relationship. If the presence of underlying dependency symptoms is not taken into account by the clinician, dependency can easily arise. However, the tendency toward dependency is not a function of hypnosis. It is a function of the client's personality structure and how the clinician and client define their relationship.

In fact, hypnosis can be used to encourage dependency, just as the therapy relationship itself can encourage dependency if it is not well managed. It is of particular importance in treating depressed clients that the clinician remain cognizant of the fact that often depression involves the client's feeling helpless and hopeless while manifesting an external locus of control (Beck et al., 1985, 1990; Seligman, 1989, 1990). It is the clinician's responsibility, therefore, to make sure that hypnosis is utilized with the goal of fostering self-reliance in the most realistic ways possible, and with great sensitivity to the specific context of the client's life.

Hypnosis Will Precipitate Suicide

As discussed in the previous chapter, a primary criticism of hypnosis relative to the treatment of depressed individuals concerns the fear that it will precipitate suicide. This is sheer myth. Hypnosis does not strip away defenses, it does not dissolve ego boundaries, it does not dissolve impulse control, nor does it create or amplify the hopelessness that is at the core of suicidal tendencies. Suicide has been called the "permanent solution to temporary problems." It reflects a rigid belief about the hopelessness of the future. If hypnosis were to be used to amplify feelings of hopelessness, then the likelihood of suicide would increase. However, if hypnosis is used to diminish feelings of hopelessness and establish stronger feelings of hopefulness, the likelihood of suicide is diminished. Consider what any experienced clinician, ostensibly not using hypnosis, would say to a suicidal client that is meant to reduce or take away the suicidal thoughts and feelings. Can you identify what is hypnotic about what might be said in such instances?

Clarke and Jackson (1983) also addressed the myth that hypnosis precipitates suicide:

Clinical folklore has it that hypnosis is contraindicated in depressed subjects. The assumption is that the experience of hypnosis will incline the depressed patient toward suicidal thoughts and actions. The incidence of suicide is known to be much higher in depression than in any other problem (Beck, 1967), but there is no evidence that hypnosis in any way causes this already high risk to be increased still further. If a piecemeal attack is made on any one facet of a clinical syndrome without regard to the treatment of the overall problem, it can raise the possibility of sudden unintended and unexpected changes in other areas of the patient's functioning. In saying this we in no way imply the acceptance of the doctrine of symptom substitution but are merely calling attention to the complex ramifications of any treatment maneuver. Thus, and to state the obvious, using hypnosis in the treatment of depression would not obviate the need to sensible recourse to anti-depressant medication. (p. 12)

These authors promote a viewpoint I find refreshingly responsible. It is their perspective that it is not hypnosis that is dangerous, but hypnosis that is misapplied.

Hypnosis Is Symptom-Oriented Treatment Generating Temporary Results

Hypnosis may be used symptomatically (to suggest away symptoms) or dynamically (to resolve underlying issues). The manner in which a clinician employs hypnosis is typically a product of personal choice and personal training. There is no particular value judgment placed on symptomatic versus dynamic hypnosis, in my view, despite my awareness that there are dynamic psychotherapists who consider anything other than long-term, insight-oriented psychodynamic therapy as superficial. In fact, change can and does occur in the absence of insight; insight is not a necessary and sufficient condition for change to occur.

The concern about the results of hypnosis being transient is legitimate, until one looks at the matter more closely. No therapy can be considered successful and no therapeutic tool can be considered valuable if they generate only transient results. Why does this misconception exist regarding hypnosis? The answer is a complex one that involves two primary variables. First, simply suggesting away symptoms may serve as a pattern interruption, but it certainly does not represent the second aspect of my definition of psychotherapy—namely, pattern building. Without the establishment of new choices, suggesting away old choices further limits an already-limited client's experience. Thus, the simple use of direct suggestion is unlikely to be successful because it is so obviously incomplete.

However, the main reason that hypnotic results may be temporary has to do with contextualization. It is now understood that hypnotic experiences are "trance state specific," meaning that the experiences generated during the hypnosis session are likely to remain with the client only during the trance state itself (Yapko, 1990). Thus, when the client emerges from trance and reassociates to his or her usual "waking" state, trance responses are likely to dissipate. A bridge must be established between the trance state and the waking state if there is to be a realistic expectation that results achieved in trance will be carried over into the rest of the client's life. The contextualization of responses through the use of posthypnotic suggestion is essential if therapeutic results are to have any lasting effect.

How long can a hypnotic suggestion last? That question can be answered with another question: How long can a useful idea last? A good hypnotic session, involving appropriate suggestions for contextualization, can yield positive results that last a lifetime.

Hypnosis Encourages Symptom Substitution

Symptom substitution refers to the onset of a new symptom, perhaps one even worse than the original, in the place of the old symptom that was removed (ostensibly) during hypnotic treatment. To assume that hypnosis creates symptom substitution, one would have to view hypnosis as only a symptomatic treatment that does not consider underlying dynamics or patterns. Hypnosis *can* be used symptomatically (direct suggestions and scripted approaches reflect this), but its most effective uses address both the underlying issues and the individual patterns that those issues encourage.

Hypnosis is sometimes dismissed as a superficial form of treatment on the basis that the complexity of underlying issues demands that they be identified and dealt with insightfully through conscious awareness and expression. However, an experienced clinician who uses hypnosis may very well recognize underlying issues and patterns and yet may choose to address them in the absence of insight. Thus, treatment can be as dynamically oriented as that of a more traditional clinician, but without a premium being placed on conscious understanding and emotional ventilation. In fact, dynamic interpretations meant to facilitate insight may even be antitherapeutic in the case of depression. Such interpretations tend to be abstract and not easily understood by concrete thinkers. It is my contention that in treating depressives, the more symbolic or metaphorical an intervention, the less effective it will be. In later chapters, I discuss the use of metaphors and of historical approaches emphasizing insights about the past, suggesting that such approaches are generally contraindicated in the treatment of depressives. For now, suffice it to say that symptom substitution is not a legitimate concern when hypnosis is skillfully applied to the salient aspects of the client's experience.

HYPNOSIS AND THERAPEUTIC CHOICES

Hypnosis permits a wide range of choices regarding where and how to intervene in the client's problems. Emphasis has been placed on a utilization approach that entails adapting one's style of intervention to the specific patterns evident in the client, rather than attempting to adapt the client to some preconceived and personally preferred theoretical and practical orientation. This affords the clinician the widest range of interventions possible as appropriate—cognitive therapy, behavioral therapy, and so forth. To facilitate the ability to tailor treatment to the individual patterns evident in the client is the essential goal of this book.

4

Hypnotic Aspects of Nonhypnotic Therapies

Considering the enormous influence that hypnosis has had on the field of psychotherapy from its beginnings, it is ironic that it has become a separate domain, seemingly distinct from the mainstream practice of psychotherapy. Hypnosis was at the base of Freud's formulations about the unconscious mind and the purposeful nature of symptoms. Hypnosis led to an in-depth understanding of the phenomenon of placebo and the role of expectations in eventual therapeutic outcomes. Hypnosis amplified awareness of and research into the mysteries of the mind by forever confounding observers in their attempts to explain such enigmatic phenomena as dissociation and suggested anesthesias.

In sum, although hypnosis has played a vital role in our (limited) understanding of the human mind, as psychotherapy has become more diversified, hypnosis has been relegated to a position of an esoteric approach unrelated to general therapeutic practice. Why is this so?

PATHS TO HYPNOTIC SEPARATISM

First, hypnosis traditionally has been viewed as an entirely intrapersonal phenomenon, as were people's symptoms, which led to the belief that only some "special" individuals were capable of experiencing it meaningfully. As a result, standardized suggestibility tests became an important part of clinical practice in order to find out who had this special gift, and to what extent (Weitzenhoffer, 1989; Spiegel & Spiegel, 1978). Thus, instead of hypnosis being viewed interpersonally, as we now know we must (at least in part), it was limited to a peculiarly intrapersonal viewpoint (Erickson & Rossi, 1979; Haley, 1973; Gilligan, 1982).

Second, the field of hypnosis was characterized by a rigid and ritualistic technique that relied on the repetition of "magical" incantations, such as: "sleep . . . deeper . . . relax . . . relax . . . relax." For as long as people held the perspective that there was something magical about the words themselves (in the absence of relevant knowledge about the idiosyncrasies of the client's information-processing style and world view), such approaches could and did flourish, as evidenced by the extraordinary amount of literature generated in previous decades that routinely featured scripted incantations.

Third, because the rest of the psychotherapy field was also limited to an intrapsychic viewpoint of people's problems, in a manner consistent with Freud's original formulations, hypnosis could easily be viewed as contraindicated when the patient's underlying psychodynamics might lead to a poor response to direct and authoritarian hypnosis. (Consider the previous two chapters' discussion of hypnosis leading to dependency, suicide, and psychosis.) It is understandable that psychotherapists exposed to this point of view would be reluctant to practice hypnosis as a ritual that attempts to either bypass or short-circuit a patient's defenses, and that voluminous warnings were issued about the dangers of using hypnosis with depressed patients. It thus becomes readily apparent from reviewing the literature on both hypnosis and depression how the field of hypnosis has come to find itself relatively isolated from mainstream psychotherapy.

When one is familiar with the concepts and patterns of clinical hypnosis, it is easier to understand how various therapies are able to generate the therapeutic results they achieve. However, in the same way that hypnosis has become separate from mainstream psychotherapy, so have the various hypnotic patterns become dissociated from the field of hypnosis as they are "begged, borrowed, and stolen" by other therapeutic modalities that "claim" them as their own (Rossi, 1987; Zeig, 1987).

The main point of this chapter is that the patterns of hypnosis are the same patterns that are applied in all schools of psychotherapy to one degree or another, generally without ever being considered hypnotic within those various schools. It seems important to recognize the presence of hypnotic concepts and techniques in various psychotherapeutic methods if we are to arrive at an understanding of what makes therapy therapeutic. That hypnotic techniques have become separate from the field of hypnosis and integrated into diverse schools of psychotherapy was certainly to be expected as we evolved a greater understanding of the role of communication in the therapy process (Rossi, 1985; Watzlawick, 1985). If one does not recognize the hypnotic aspects of one's communications that are intended to be therapeutic, then the opportunity to use such patterns in deliberate and skillful ways decreases.

In Chapter 3, a distinction is made between formal and informal hypnosis. Formal hypnotic procedures are described as necessarily involving an overt introduction of the word "hypnosis" to the client ("We are going to do hypnosis now. Sit down and make yourself comfortable."). Informal hypnosis is defined as the use of influential communications designed to elicit hypnotic (i.e., focused and nonvolitional) responses in the absence of a formal induction. Informal hypnosis, therefore, can be thought of as being present wherever effective communication takes place. Hypnotic responses not only are possible, but are quite routine, even in the absence of any formal hypnotic induction (Watzlawick, 1985; Zeig, 1980a).

HYPNOTIC PHENOMENA IN THERAPY

If we consider some of the most basic psychotherapeutic models and how hypnotic patterns are evident within them, the point of this chapter becomes immediately clear. For example, traditional psychoanalytic and psychodynamic approaches place a large premium on "working through" childhood issues (i.e., lifting childhood repression, resolving unresolved issues, facilitating transference to the therapist of feelings toward significant authorities of childhood). It is a constant aspect of such approaches to emphasize insight into and clarity about one's past experiences. The use of techniques designed to enhance recall (called hypermnesia), and even to encourage the reliving of significant childhood experiences (called revivification), represents an entire category of hypnotic techniques that relate to the classical trance phenomenon known as "age regression."

In Gestalt therapy, emphasis is placed on identifying "here and now" experiences and establishing communication with different "parts" of one's self (i.e., polarities, feelings). The clinician plays an active role in suggesting frequent "dissociations," a classical trance phenomenon, in order to be able to identify and directly address those various parts. Likewise, rehearsing conversations with an unavailable significant other to the extent of intensely imagining him or her sitting in an empty chair across from one involves another trance phenomenon; that is, "positive hallucinations."

Cognitive therapy emphasizes orderly thinking and rationality, and, in so doing, it makes use of various hypnotic patterns, including the dissociations encouraged for the purpose of separating thoughts from feelings and the dissociative accessing of the mechanisms that generate "automatic" (unconscious) thoughts.

Interpersonal psychotherapy puts great value on the therapeutic relationship as a means of fostering the client's self-exploration and expression of feelings. It also makes use of posthypnotic suggestions in order to place important learnings in relevant contexts. Such strategies involve hypnotic "age progression." Interpersonal psychotherapy also advocates the most fundamental hypnotic strategy of all: the acceptance and use of the client's experience, which is the foundation for the utilization model of hypnosis presented in this book.

Each model for treating depression in particular, and each model of psychotherapy in general, has its associated self-defining concepts and techniques. In any case, the model's important points must be *communicated* to the client in such a way that the client can make pragmatic use of what the clinician has to teach. It is at this level, the communication level, that we can identify the hypnotic characteristics of every psychotherapy (Watzlawick, 1985). Thus, in this chapter, I identify how aspects of hypnosis can be observed in the most commonly employed methods for treating depressed clients. Therapy techniques are significant in terms of their potential to help, but only through a sensitive and well-tailored approach can these techniques be of any benefit to the client. Technique *always* exists in some context, and the role of context is the hypnotic framework defining the technique's potential usefulness.

Previously, I placed great emphasis on the value of structure in treatment (i.e., how) rather than on content (i.e., what). Let us consider the subjective experience of the depressed client. Hypno-

sis provides insight into the phenomenology of depression, allowing us to see how hypnotic patterns are, in fact, the mechanism
for the creation of experience. Hypnosis is a framework for better
understanding subjective experience in general, and depression in
particular.

WHAT MAKES HYPNOSIS HYPNOTIC?

What makes an intervention hypnotic? This question is as difficult
to answer as the question, "What makes an intervention therapeutic?" After almost a full century of the continuous practice of psychotherapy, the question remains just that—a question. There are
those who emphasize the relationship with a caring and empathetic
therapist as the foundation for successful psychotherapy; others
stress the value of new information in promoting therapeutic
change; and still others suggest that it is the environment of open
expressiveness that proves to be therapeutic. To some extent, all of
these are important aspects of treatment, but the point remains that
all of the specific factors that constitute effective therapy are not yet
fully defined. There is a wide diversity of thought and practice by
clinicians who emphasize their own subjective viewpoints (including
me), which makes precise shared definitions difficult. The elements
that make an intervention hypnotic or therapeutic may be difficult
to define, but they clearly lie beyond mere technique. Many individuals, for example, who practice hypnosis are not particularly hypnotic in their methods. Likewise, many who do therapy are not
particularly therapeutic. Doing therapy is not the same as being therapeutic, nor is doing hypnosis the same as being hypnotic. What
characteristics define an intervention as hypnotic? How can one identify the presence of hypnosis in therapies that have never been considered hypnotic?

The factors that make an intervention hypnotic are generally
reflected in the communications exchanged and the consequences
of those communications between clinician and client. An intervention may be considered hypnotic when it involves the presence of an
ambiguously defined—and not necessarily formally induced—state
called "trance," for lack of a better term, although some prefer
describing the client as being "in hypnosis." The term trance is

meant to describe a client's enhanced state of focus (i.e., concentrated attention) that has certain important characteristics:

1. Trance is characterized by a state of experiential absorption. The client in trance is employing a mechanism of selective attention in which his or her attention is focused on a specific stimulus or set of associations that the person experiences as absorbing.

2. The trance is characterized by some degree of dissociation in which the client experiences himself or herself as removed from his or her usual frame of reference.

3. The client has suspended the ongoing process of reality testing, permitting him or her to respond to suggested realities in an experiential, nonrational way.

4. The trance experience affords a client the opportunity for an amplification and utilization of resources within, which are usually considered by the individual to be outside the realm of his or her "normal" consciousness. These so-called "unconscious resources" are the main catalyst for therapeutic change in the utilization framework. The ability to make use of aspects of the client's experience to which he or she normally does not relate in any meaningful way is one of the most significant reasons for integrating hypnosis into one's intervention.

5. Hypnosis necessarily involves, just as any psychotherapeutic tool must, a reassociation of the client's inner world. Hypnosis in and of itself is not the therapeutic agent; rather, it is the associations stimulated by the hypnotic experience that form the basis for therapeutic change in the client's experience.

6. Hypnosis occurs in an interpersonal context, just as psychotherapy does. Therefore, the quality of the client's relationship with the clinician is a critical factor. The process of interpersonal influence is clearly a multidimensional process that involves conscious and unconscious aspects that exist on personal, interpersonal, and situational levels.

Thus, for an intervention to be considered hypnotic, it must address these personal, interpersonal, and situational variables in such a way so as to maximize therapeutic dissociations and reassociations of experience.

HYPNOSIS AS A CATALYST

Hypnosis is a part of other psychotherapies, and it is not a therapy in and of itself. It involves a style of communication, a way of thinking about a therapeutic relationship, and a sensitivity to the client's specific way of being in the world. Integral to an understanding of this book is an understanding of hypnosis as a mechanism embedded within all psychotherapies that can be readily identified as a catalyst for therapeutic change when therapy is successful. When therapy is not successful, or even is antitherapeutic, hypnosis can be recognized as a factor in the failure; "wrong" aspects of the client's experience were amplified or hurtful associations were established.

Hypnosis, like therapy, cannot be practiced effectively within a rigid formula-bound framework. Thus, all hypnosis is not alike. It is perhaps easiest to differentiate among the types of hypnosis according to how the hypnosis is applied. Hypnosis used for entertainment purposes represents a different application of hypnotic principles than when it is used in a clinical context. Techniques found in a research or experimental context may reflect a conceptualization of hypnosis that parallels clinical conceptualizations, yet experimental methods must be adapted extensively before they will have any applicability in clinical interaction. This important point highlights the fact that hypnosis that has been conceptualized and practiced by someone with a psychodynamic orientation is going to be fundamentally different than the hypnosis used by someone in a cognitive or interpersonal therapy framework. Yet within all approaches, hypnosis catalyzes experiential absorption, dissociation, responsiveness to the clinician's guidance, focus on suggested associations, and, ultimately, a reassociation of the client's inner world.

Hypnosis is clearly identifiable as a significant element in any psychotherapy when we recognize the roles of suggestion, expectation, and influential communication in the therapeutic relationship (Haley, 1973). The goal of any therapy is to influence the client in such a way that the client will discover new ways of experiencing himself or herself that are deemed desirable. In this respect, the therapeutic relationship is the vital context in which hypnosis and therapy occur; regardless of one's preferred style of intervention, it is what one says and does to which the client responds (consciously and unconsciously) that eventually determine what becomes possible for the client.

It is well recognized that human beings experience the world on at least two dimensions: the symbolic and the empirical. When presenting for treatment, the client is experiencing unpleasant associations and experiences on an empirical level—the level of actual sensory experience. But in order for the clinician to have some understanding of the client's experience, the client must describe it by making use of symbolic representations known as "words." Words are simply symbols for experience; they are not the experiences themselves. Both the client and the clinician communicate symbolically through words. Thus, there is a constant shifting back and forth between empirical and symbolic levels of experience and between clinician and client.

Hypnosis is the common denominator, defining the "how" of how each therapy is able to generate meaningful therapeutic results. Each therapy relies on patterns of influential communication to establish new associations in the client's inner world. In analyzing short transcripts from leading cognitive therapy practitioners presented later in this chapter, you will see how the practitioners make use of hypnotic patterning, which is generally invisible to the practitioner unfamiliar with hypnosis. This lack of familiarity may lead one to believe that it is the technique itself, rather than its associated hypnotic elements, that is responsible for changing the client's experience.

EVIDENCE OF HYPNOSIS IN COGNITIVE-THERAPY

Sample Transcripts

Hypnosis amplifies and deamplifies portions of experience selectively. How valuable a given intervention is ultimately depends on the outcome. In that respect, the purpose or intention of a technique is only important to the extent that the purpose has been realized through the intervention. In order for the technique to be useful, it must be structurally sound and contextually and relationally appropriate. The point is that what makes the clinician's communication meaningful is not the structure or the content of the communication itself, but how that structure and content are perceived by the client. When the client cannot relate meaningfully to what the clinician has said, or does not find it relevant or useful, or when the client associates to the clinician's communications in a way that produces an unexpected and undesirable outcome—these are the things that make an intervention antitherapeutic.

The next section of this chapter contains portions of three cognitive therapy transcripts published as samples of the approach in a leading work on the treatment of depression, Beck et al.'s *Cognitive Therapy of Depression* (1979). The cognitive model is, arguably, the leading psychotherapy for depression, and as such, it provides a good reference point for identifying the associated hypnotic patterns in an approach not generally regarded as hypnotic.

In these transcripts are communications intended to be therapeutic for the client. Although the transcripts reflect important techniques and conceptual points about the treatment of depression in general, special consideration will be given to how hypnotic patterns are evident within the therapeutic techniques. Commentary and analysis are provided following each communication to identify what the communication suggested from the hypnotic standpoint and how it was useful for that context.

The Transcripts with Commentary and Analysis

Cognitive Rehearsal (Beck et al., 1979; p. 136)

Therapist: So you agree that it would be a good idea to go to an exercise class.	Establishing rapport through the use of a "Yes Set" (O'Hanlon, 1987).
Patient: Yes, I always feel good after them.	Acceptance of "Yes Set"; accessing and amplifying associated feelings.
T: Okay, well I'd like you to use your imagination and go through each step involved in getting to the class.	Direct suggestion to associate the good feelings to the behavioral sequence of going to class.
P: Well, I'll just have to go the way I've always gone.	Accessing via spontaneous age regression past ineffective sequence.

T: I think we need to be more specific. We know that you've decided to go to class before but everytime you've run into some roadblocks. Let's go over each step and see what might interfere with getting to class. I'd like you to go through all of the steps needed to get to your class. Go over each step in your imagination and tell me what they are.

Shifting from age regression to age progression; orienting the client internally to full, detailed representation of current associations to future sequence before intervention. Direct suggestion to verbalize content of the sequence and associations.

P: Okay. I know what you mean.

Accepts the suggestion to age progress and verbalize.

T: The class starts at 9 a.m. What time should we start?

Anchoring the unchangeable pivot point on which the new behavioral sequence must rest. Associates self (via "we") to the new sequence as external support for facilitating integration.

P: About 7:30. I'll wake up to the alarm and probably be feeling lousy. I always hate starting the day.

Age progresses to identify the auditory anchor (association) which initiates the new behavioral sequence; identifies a negative kinesthetic (emotional) association both to the alarm and time of day.

T: How can you handle that problem?

Presupposition that those associations can be interrupted, and an indirect suggestion (injunction) to do so by means unspecified (process suggestion).

P: Well, that's why I'll give myself extra time. I'll start by getting dressed and having breakfast. Then, I'll pick up my equipment .... (pause). ... Oh, oh, wait, I don't have a pair of shorts to wear. That's one roadblock.

Identifies the resource of "extra time" as the means for shifting previous negative internal associations; in doing so, reassociate new feelings of comfort to the alarm and morning hour. Now is able to shift to behavioral focus, rather than affective. Continues sequence and identifies concrete detail needing attention.

T: What can you do to solve that problem?	Presupposition that problem can be solved; indirect suggestion to do so independently via process (unspecified) suggestion regarding strategy.
P: Well, I can go out and buy some.	Accepts suggestions and resolves concern.
T: Can you visualize that? What comes next?	Reaffirms solution, anchors it visually, facilitating some dissociation from affect. Suggests continuing the sequence.
P: I picture myself all ready to go and the car isn't there.	Accepts suggestion for visual representation, identifies next concrete problem.
T: What can you do about it?	Presupposition that problem can be solved; indirect suggestion to do so independently via process suggestion regarding strategy.
P: I'll ask my husband to bring the car early.	Identifies a solution independently.
T: What do you picture next?	Suggestion to continue visual sequencing of age progressed behavior.
P: I'm driving to the class and I decide to turn round and go back.	Notice the shift out of future tense into present and the immediacy of the unpleasant kinesthetic associations which block continuation of the behavioral sequence.
T: Why?	Direct suggestion to identify the associated feelings.
P: Because I think I'll look foolish.	Current feelings of inadequacy are identified as associated to future images of carrying out the new behavioral sequence.
T: What's the answer to that?	Presupposition that the feelings can be redirected, and therapy dissociated from the new behavioral sequence. Indirect suggestion to do so.

P: Well, actually the other people are just interested in the exercise, not in how anybody looks.

Dissociation is accomplished; feelings are split from carrying out the behavioral sequence while the shift from internal feelings of self-consciousness to the focus on exercise is accomplished.

In a note following the transcript, Beck et al. (1979) reported:

She was then asked to rehearse the entire sequence again and this time was able to *imagine the various steps without any interfering cognitions* [italics the author's]. Subsequently, she indeed drove to the class and did not experience any difficulties. (pp. 136–137)

This transcript showed the therapeutic value of using concretely and linearly structured suggestions, including process suggestions, direct suggestions, presuppositions, and indirect suggestions. Age progression and dissociation are used as mechanisms to facilitate integration of the new behavioral sequence.

Assumptions as Self-Fulfilling Prophesies (Beck et al., 1979; p. 260)

Patient: Not being loved leads automatically to unhappiness.

Patient identifies the dysfunctional emotional association (i.e., unhappiness) to the cognitive perception (i.e., not being loved) that must be interrupted.

Therapist: Not being loved is a "nonevent." How can a nonevent lead automatically to something?

Reframing meaning of "not being loved," which begins the dissociation of affect from its perceived existence.

P: I just don't believe anyone could be happy without being loved.

Shifts from personal and specific to impersonal, global generalization, which would have been difficult, if not impossible, to address effectively.

T: This is your belief. If you believe something, this belief will dictate your emotional reactions.

Shifts right back to personal and specific ("This is your belief"). Establishes association between beliefs and feelings via direct and process suggestions.

P: I don't understand that.

Feedback that no meaningful association was successfully established in the client's awareness.

T: If you believe something, you're going to act and feel as if it were true, whether it is or not.

A direct suggestion is given that associates thoughts and feelings. Indirect suggestion to orient to future contexts where thoughts will influence feelings, and associate feelings of doubt as to their accuracy.

P: You mean, if I believe I'll be unhappy without love, it's only my belief causing my unhappiness?

Client orients to a current and future stable belief, and begins to distance (dissociate) from its influence ("*only my belief . . .* "[italics the author's]) on his feelings.

T: And when you feel unhappy, you probably say to yourself, "See, I was right. If I don't have love, I am bound to be unhappy."

Shift from process to content suggestion encouraging the auditory associational link between the specific thoughts and their associated feelings. They are framed as inaccurate representations, thereby encouraging via indirect, process suggestions a dissociation from them and a reassociation of different feelings.

P: How can I get out of this trap?

The client accesses no resources enabling him to comply with the indirect and process suggestions to reassociate his feelings.

T: You could experiment with your belief about having to be loved. Force yourself to suspend this belief and see what happens. Pay attention to the natural consequences of

Dissociation via experimentation (indirectly suggesting a more objective view) is employed. A shift from an internal focus on feelings to an internal focus on images is sug-

not being loved, not the consequences created by your belief. For example, can you picture yourself on a tropical island with all the delicious fruits and other food available?

gested, interrupting the client's pattern. An additional suggestion to focus on competing kinesthetics— namely, delicious fruits—is also given, further interrupting the client's usual pattern.

P: Yes, it looks pretty good.

Response in a visual mode, an alternate focus from his feelings, thereby dissociating from them.

T: Now, imagine that there are primitive people on the island. They are friendly and helpful, but they do not love you. None of them loves you.

More content suggestions for enhanced imagery and dissociation from his usual frame of reference. Reassociates comfortable feelings to impersonal images of nonloving people, who are framed as "primitive," interrupting patterns of devaluing self.

P: I can picture that.

Accepts imagery suggestions and associated injunctions, dissociating from his usual frame of reference.

T: How do you feel in your fantasy?

Shift to immediacy of kinesthetic experience to amplify awareness for its having changed, indirectly suggesting the new association of comfort to the old context of perceiving not being loved.

P: Relaxed and comfortable.

Suggestion to amplify new kinesthetic awareness is accepted.

T: So you can see that it does not necessarily follow that if you aren't loved, you will be unhappy.

Therapist directly suggests associating the new feeling of comfort to the old context of perceiving not being loved (posthypnotic suggestion).

In this transcript, the therapist uses direct, indirect, process, content, positive, and posthypnotic suggestions. Dissociation, imagery, attentional shifts, and reframing are employed as mechanisms to catalyze the therapeutic intervention.

Providing a Rationale for Doing Homework (Beck et al., 1979; pp. 274-5)

Therapist: I'd like to have you count on a wrist counter the number of times you say "should" to yourself this week. What do you think of the idea?

Direct suggestion to implement a behavioral directive. Indirect suggestion to dissociate dysfunctional emotional associations to the word "should" and reassociate adaptive cognitive or affective associations.

Patient: It sounds a little stupid to me. Why would I want to do that?

Patient associates no sense of purposefulness to the assignment, therefore judging it "stupid." Highlights association between purposefulness and cooperation.

T: We've found that counting automatic negative thoughts makes one more aware of them and thus easier to answer. Also, merely counting tends to decrease their influence. (The therapist might also say, "Recording helps put distance between yourself and your thoughts, and gives you feedback and evaluation in changing thoughts.")

Amplifies the value of self-awareness and builds an association between self-awareness and feeling better. The alternate response offered in parentheses is actually the more powerful response in its direct suggestions for dissociation, both of self from thoughts and of thoughts from feelings. Establishes a future orientation (age progression) that relief will follow the suggested dissociations.

P: I don't think this will work for me.

The client identifies that he cannot access the resources necessary to accomplish the dissociation, associating current negative feelings to the (future) carrying out of the directive, establishing a negative, demotivating expectation.

T: I'm glad you are questioning me. This shows you are using your reasoning powers. There is no reason you should automatically believe something just because I say it. I'm not positive this will work in your case, but I have a hunch—or a *hypothesis*, to give it a scientific

Though the client did not actually question the therapist, the therapist reframes the client's negative expectation as questioning. This is a positive framing, redefining and establishing, therefore, a healthier emotional reassociation to the client's response. This reframing

sound—that it will work. I'd like to test this hypothesis out.

paves the way for the utilization of the client's feelings, rather than discounting them. Such redefinition of resistance as cooperation is a fundamental utilization technique, and rather than confront or interpret the resistance, it is even encouraged as the necessary precursor to positive change. Furthermore, such a reframe of client doubt encourages a shift from an external locus of control (having to comply with the therapist) to an internal one (choosing to participate collaboratively). Introduction via negative suggestion of the word "hypothesis" provides an affective dissociational cue, indirectly suggesting objective experimentation rather than subjective focus on feelings, a pattern interruption.

P: What do you mean, "test your hypothesis"?

The client has no meaningful association to the phrase.

T: I have a hypothesis that it will help you and you have a hypothesis that it won't. I don't know for sure who is right. Do you?

The therapist indirectly suggests that the client may be wrong while directly suggesting he believes there is a value in suspending judgment—dissociating from personal feelings or bias—in order to experiment. The indirect suggestion to the client is that his view of reality may be distorted, associating feelings of uncertainty to his perspectives. Suggests establishing an "I Don't Know Response Set" (Erickson & Rossi, 1981) to build responsiveness (confusion).

P: No, I don't.

The client accepts his lack of knowledge, a precursor to obtaining compliance.

T: I suggest we run an experiment for a week, gather some data, and see which point of view conforms more closely to the facts. How does that sound to you?

The therapist reintroduces the directive with all the new emotional associations likely to lead the client to comply established. Indirect suggestion to age progress over the next week with associated images of carrying out the experiment (posthypnotic suggestions).

In this transcript, the therapist uses direct, indirect, process, positive, negative, and posthypnotic suggestions. Dissociation, age progression, reframing, utilization of resistance, and confusion are utilized to achieve the goal of obtaining compliance for the assigned directive.

HYPNOSIS IN COMMON TECHNIQUES FOR TREATING DEPRESSION

Hypnosis has been described in general terms as a basis for amplifying or deamplifying, and dissociating or associating, elements of a client's experience. In the same way that hypnotic patterns were evident in the cognitive therapy methods presented in the previous section, so are they evident in any therapeutic intervention. The list of specific techniques described in the literature on depression is far too extensive to consider fully here. However, by identifying some of the most common techniques of intervention, the reader can become better acquainted with the various ways that hypnotic patterns may be evident in them.

Hypnosis in Cognitive Therapy

Nezu, Nezu, and Perri (1989) described numerous techniques of problem solving for depression and categorized them as follows: modeling, behavioral rehearsal, homework assignments, reinforcement, and feedback. Each of these methods involves experiential learning. For example, modeling can be done indirectly through filmed or pictorial presentation, but may be accomplished best through role-playing procedures in which the clinician demonstrates to the client what an effective response to a particular problematic context might be. The use of behavioral rehearsal techniques involves actually placing the client in a particular context in order to establish a new behavioral sequence within that context. The mere fact of the rehearsal itself establishes an associational link between a particular context and a particular sequence of behavior. Consider the cognitive rehearsal transcribed in the previous section as a parallel example. Homework assignments in the problem solving approach are considered to be an important feature of overall treatment. They involve an amplification of relevant learnings in contexts outside the therapeutic relationship, thereby increasing the likelihood of being able to establish appropriate associations to a wider variety of contexts.

In the cognitive therapy model as described by Beck (1967, 1987; Beck et al., 1979), the cognitive therapy techniques include increasing the client's awareness of his or her "automatic thoughts." Beck is clearly comfortable with the term "automatic thoughts," which, from a hypnotic point of view, certainly reflects an appreciation of powerful unconscious information processing. Beck's primary goal is to bring the automatic thoughts into the client's conscious awareness in order to create the possibility of successful refutation (Beck, 1987). Certainly, from the hypnotic standpoint, it represents a pattern interruption to take unconscious material and make it not only conscious, but the object of active conscious refutation.

Beck (1987) describes as the next most important aspect of cognitive therapy the client's recognition of his or her cognitive errors. This step represents a selective amplification of the cognitive element of the client's experience. By focusing on the cognitive aspects, one necessarily lessens focuses on affective or any other aspects of experience. In other words, the client is encouraged to represent his or her subjective experience differently. New associations are established as the client makes the transition from being highly focused on emotional experience to becoming focused on the cognitive realm of experience.

Beck (1987) then emphasizes a fundamental component of the therapy process that he calls "reality testing though collaborative empiricism" (p. 156). He again underscores the value of experiential learning as opposed to simply providing cognitive instruction. He speculates that a common denominator of all psychotherapies that may be the basis for therapeutic change is what he calls a "corrective emotional experience" (p. 159). Reality testing through collaborative empiricism means, in essence, creating a context in which the client can determine whether his or her perspective about some particular dimension of experience is a reasonably accurate or useful one.

By involving the client in experiential learning, a deeper representational shift can take place. The client no longer is immersed in only an emotion or a cognition, but is now immersed in a broader range of experiences in which the rigid parameters of his or her beliefs or feelings are collapsed. There is greater opportunity, therefore, for an experiential absorption (i.e., therapeutic trance) in an experience that fundamentally shifts one's internal representations.

Beck describes the most common cognitive therapy techniques as activity scheduling and graded task assignments (including behavioral rehearsal and in-session cognitive rehearsals or imagery exercises). In activity scheduling, the typically passive depressed client actively creates experiences to amplify portions of experience to which he or she normally does not attend. The directive is, in essence, to "do something different." The expectation is communicated in a hypnotically suggestive way that by doing things differently, the client's experience will be different. The direct and indirect suggestions are established that depression is a by-product, at least in part, of what one does, and that for depression to lift, one needs to do things differently. The corollary suggestion is implicit (and perhaps explicit, as well) that action leads to change.

As for the graded task assignments, the value of behavioral rehearsal is fundamental to both hypnotic experience and cognitive therapy. It is unrealistic to expect that the client can immediately become congruent and fluent in an entirely new pattern that is far beyond the range of his or her previous experience. In fact, in the realm of clinical hypnosis, great attention is paid to the establishment of what is known as the "response set"; that is, the establishment of the momentum of response on the part of the client (Erickson & Rossi, 1981; O'Hanlon, 1987; Yapko, 1990). The client is not expected to be able to experience an age regression or any other suggested trance phenomenon immediately. Rather, care must be taken to establish a mind-set on a gradual basis, immersing the client in the experience to an increasingly greater extent as time goes on. The behavioral rehearsal methods of cognitive therapy are similarly structured, allowing gradual immersion in a new behavioral framework and, consequently, in the associated cognitive and emotional frameworks as well. Behavioral rehearsal permits clients to step outside their usual frames of reference, which is hypnotic in itself, and thereby immerse themselves in an altered reality.

Perhaps the most obvious example of hypnotic methodology within cognitive therapy is the heavy reliance on the use of cognitive rehearsal techniques, also known as visualization or visual imagery. Imagery is a staple of the cognitive approaches. The client is instructed to imagine himself or herself in whatever context has proved difficult. The client has the opportunity to visualize responding to circumstances differently, establishing a new association hypnotically through the mechanism of posthypnotic suggestion. In the first transcript in the previous section, note Beck et al.'s (1979) postsession description: "She . . . was able to imagine the various steps without any interfering cognitions"(p. 137). This is precisely the description and effect of a posthypnotic suggestion. By definition, a posthypnotic suggestion is a suggestion implanted during the course of the hypnotic procedure regarding some experience the client is to have in some other context later, ostensibly outside the parameters of the hypnotic interaction (Yapko, 1990). Whenever a therapist says to his or her client, "When you're in situation X that used to be troublesome for you, you will now be able to handle it effectively by doing Y and Z," he or she is utilizing the classic structure of posthypnotic suggestions.

Beck et al. (1979) describe numerous other techniques that are widely employed in cognitive therapy approaches that can also be described in the hypnotic framework:

Self-observation in recording of one's thoughts (p. 146) to interrupt and identify unconscious patterns

The use of imagery (p. 148) to establish new contextual associations

The use of worst-case scenarios (p. 154) to dissociate affect from experience

The use of reattribution (p. 157) to dissociate affect from cognition

The use of the wrist counter (p. 165) to redirect attention and dissociate affect from context

The use of humor (p. 172) to reframe meanings and redirect associated affect

The use of excessive focus on one's feelings (p. 173) to facilitate affective dissociations

Inducing anger (p. 171) to facilitate reassociation of affect to context

Cognitive therapist David Burns (1980) makes use of all of Beck's techniques, in addition to other techniques, including:

A "Triple Column Technique" (p. 60) to dissociate affect from context

The cost–benefit analysis (p. 150) to encourage dissociation and age progression by anticipating consequences and dissociating from the immediate context

The daily activity schedule (p. 88) to reassociate positive affect to life experience

Each of these techniques has hypnotic aspects that catalyze its effectiveness.

Hypnosis in Interpersonal Therapy

The interpersonal psychotherapy model (IPT) emphasizes, in particular, the relationship and systemic dimensions of the depressed client's condition. Klerman et al. (1984) describe a number of techniques as fundamental to the IPT model, all of which clearly reflect hypnotic patterning, including: (1) exploratory techniques, (2) clarification, (3) encouragement of affect, (4) communication analysis, and (5) directive techniques, such as the use of advice, limit-setting education, direct help, modeling, and role playing.

The exploratory techniques described in the IPT model are ways for the clinician to amplify the relevant portions of the client's experience to a degree suitable for intervention. The techniques can be either direct or indirect. The direct elicitation of client experience involves the use of hypnotic content suggestions; the client is encouraged to reveal specific pieces of information by selectively focusing on those relevant areas and verbalizing their associated content. In the nondirective exploration, the hypnotic framework of accepting and utilizing the client's experience and the use of hypnotic process suggestions (i.e., suggestions with no specific associated content) are employed to amplify awareness of the flow of client experience with minimal intrusion by the clinician.

The use of clarification techniques powerfully demonstrates the value of posthypnotic suggestions for the purpose of contextualizing the client's experience. These techniques challenge the client more clearly to establish the limits of his or her beliefs, feelings, or behaviors. The client learns to dissociate from previous patterns and to respond to what is appropriate or best in a given context.

The technique of communication analysis is used to highlight for the client the distinction between intentions and outcomes. The client is now made responsible for the quality of his or her communications— a perceptual shift—and he or she begins to learn that one's intended meaning may not necessarily be adequately communicated by the sender or properly received by the receiver. This is a powerful hypnotic reframing in that it suggests to the client that effective communication techniques are a determinant of the quality of one's relationships. It involves shifting the client's usual focus from himself or herself as being somehow personally deficient or inadequate, while directly suggesting that his or her problems are related to specific interpersonal skill deficits. A fundamental suggestion essential to the recovery of any depressed client is that the problem is not entirely within the person of the client; rather, the problem is in the (ineffective) way the client is attempting to do whatever it is he or she wants to do. This is a reframing technique to help build self-esteem.

The interpersonal psychotherapist using directive techniques might employ techniques of educating, advising, modeling, or directly helping the client solve some of the practical issues he or she faces. Although directive techniques are recognized as valuable in the interpersonal psychotherapy model, they are also viewed as not necessarily the most desirable form of intervention. Klerman et al. (1984) state:

> Optimally, with the exception of education, direct techniques should be used sparingly. They are best used in early sessions to create an atmosphere in which the therapist is perceived as a helping person . . . Too frequent use is a mistake; so are suggestions that are too specific and direct, or that undermine the

patient's sense of autonomy, or that are based on misinforma-
tion or incorrect perceptions. (pp. 151–152).

The wisdom in wanting to minimize dependency is self-evident.
It is important to provide direction in treatment only until the client
can act for himself or herself.

Other techniques associated with the IPT model are decision analysis and role playing. In decision analysis, the client is asked to consider a wide range of alternative actions and their consequences in
order to solve a particular problem. Klerman et al. (1984) describe
this as "the major action-oriented technique of interpersonal psychotherapy" (p. 152).

The technique of continually helping the client to generate a wider
variety of alternatives in responding to problem situations is a common denominator of all psychotherapies for depression. The framework in which the client lives can easily be viewed as a symptomatic
trance wherein attention is selectively focused on limited and dysfunctional options (Gilligan, 1989; Araoz, 1985). By being encouraged to consider a greater variety of viewpoints and possibilities, the
client begins to break down rigidities of perception and to establish
a new reality base that suggests that problems can be solved in a variety of ways, rather than through only one (blocked) path.

Role-playing techniques in the IPT model involve the clinician's
taking the role of some significant person in the client's life. Role
playing is used to explore the client's feelings and communication
style, and to rehearse new ways for the client to behave with others.
Clearly, when role-play is used for the purpose of exploring feelings
and communication styles, the client is being asked to regress and
act out a practiced form of previous behavior—the hypnotic process
of revivification. By asking the client to role-play possibilities the client is oriented experientially to the future, and the mechanism of
age progression then is used to establish posthypnotic suggestions
for new possible behaviors and responses.

CONCLUSION

In this chapter, I have described hypnotic patterns as the catalyst for
all therapeutic modalities. The fact that hypnosis has become disso-

ciated from the basic framework of therapy as a process of social influence has led to its being viewed as a separate, and even arbitrary, phenomenon with little relevance to the therapy process. However, this chapter has underscored the fact that not only is hypnosis relevant in the therapy process, but it is inevitably and inexorably intertwined within it. Whatever makes therapy work in whatever form it is practiced is ultimately hypnotic in nature, as was evident in the excerpted transcripts and in the techniques described, where the various hypnotic patterns lead to fundamental shifts in the way the client experiences himself or herself.

Hypnosis as a therapeutic tool can virtually never be contraindicated in the treatment of depression, or of any other disorder for that matter. How hypnosis is used to amplify or deamplify, and to dissociate or associate, portions of experience within a therapeutic strategy dictates whether the suggested experiences will be beneficial or not. Given the power and versatility of hypnosis, it is clear that those who are hypnotically trained can benefit greatly from using hypnosis in conjunction with other therapy tools, and that those who are not hypnotically trained can enhance their effectiveness by learning hypnosis.

5

Depression and Symptomatic Trances

Throughout this volume, I espouse hypnosis as a potentially valuable treatment tool, as if hypnosis were inherently good. As stated earlier, hypnosis is neither "good" nor "bad." Its value is derived from the results it generates in a given context. Consider imagery techniques, a specific form of hypnotic procedure. In imagery, the client is instructed first to develop and then to become absorbed in a series of visual images in which he or she no longer is bound by actual or perceived limitations. Instead, the client visualizes himself or herself responding to troublesome situations in a manner that produces a beneficial result. Through the process of imagery, as discussed in the last chapter, new responses (i.e., feelings, behaviors, thoughts) can become associated to the specific context focused upon in the imagery.

In the same way that imagery can be used to facilitate the client's making useful shifts in his or her responses to the context under consideration, one can easily see how imagery can also be negatively applied to generate undesirable responses. If, for example, an individual visualizes boarding an airplane and strapping himself or herself into the seat, and then the plane taking off, the engines suddenly becoming disabled, the plane rapidly crashing to earth, and, finally, twisted metal and body parts scattered over the countryside, it is easy to appreciate how such a series of images could lead one to develop a phobic response to airplanes and the experience of flying.

The mechanisms employed in the therapeutic applications of hypnosis are the identical mechanisms that can be used in antitherapeutic applications. Thus, not all therapeutic interventions are created equal. The extent to which the clinician can meaningfully absorb the client in relevant experiences that will prove beneficial is the extent to which therapy will succeed. When the clinician focuses on irrelevant or even harmful dimensions of experience, the client responds with further symptomatic experience. If viewed only intra-personally, it is easy to attribute the client's lack of progress (or even backsliding) to his or her individual psychodynamics, rather than to the nature of the intervention used by the clinician.

DEPRESSIVE REALITIES

What is it about hypnosis that so engages the client that he or she is able to experience dimensions of the self that normally are inac-cessible? Some refer to the suspension of "reality testing" as a mech-anism that encourages the client to become absorbed in the "reality" suggested by the clinician. Ernest Hilgard (1968) described the cli-ent's experience of hypnosis as believed-in imagination. In other words, the client can become so absorbed in hypnotically generated experiences that the parameters defining reality seem to diffuse to the point of invisibility. Formal trance induction need not take place in order for this to occur.

Consider the universal process of socialization. Every human being is socialized intensively by the larger culture of which he or she is a part. Through socialization, each individual forms a view of self and the universe that is relatively consistent (or, at least, not divi-sively inconsistent) with the views of the socializing agents of society. When one considers how extremely diverse the spectra of human perception and culture are, it is apparent that the range of interpre-tations of "reality" is extraordinarily broad. In this sense, Hilgard's view of hypnosis as believed-in imagination applies equally well to individual interpretations of life experience.

Consider the careers of mental health professionals. I have invested nearly two decades of my life in developing a broader and deeper understanding of human experience. My intense interest in clinical psychology is a statement about *me,* not about the worth of my chosen profession. When I conduct workshops, as I routinely do, I am powerfully reinforced by the attendees in my conviction that the mental health profession is an important one. However, I regu-larly encounter individuals whose view of reality is substantially dif-ferent from my own. Many people not only have no interest in psychology, but may even hold it in contempt! The interesting thing is that their lives can work equally well in spite of a total lack of interest in what others do for a living. Is it my believed-in imagination that leads me to believe that books like this one make a difference? And is this a useful belief?

Most readers will have had clinical training in the use of projective tests, such as the Rorschach Inkblot. The underlying mechanism in these tests is what is known as the "projective hypothesis" (Sundberg, Taplin, & Tyler, 1983), which states that when someone faces an ambiguous stimulus, he or she projects meaning onto the ambiguity that is an extension of his or her own individual frame of reference. It seems apparent that the most ambiguous stimulus that any individual faces is LIFE! Life does not have a meaning that is independent of the meaning we project onto it. This process of making projections about life experiences dictates one's overall quality of life. In the case of depression, the projections are characteristically negative, self-limiting, repetitive, self-endangering, and self-devaluing. The fundamental point here is that life is an ambiguous stimulus, and depression is, to a large extent, a predictable by-product of ongoing negative projections.

Life as an Inkblot

Life is made up of countless ambiguities. The fact that the mental health profession is so divided within itself is simply a reflection of how invested in the "believed-in imagination" theorists and practitioners are in their responses to the ambiguous stimulus of whatever disorder it is they treat. In the mental health profession, the major task is to gain some clarity and precise knowledge about the inkblots of our clients.

One cannot strive to seek "truth" in situations that are inherently ambiguous. There are no right answers to inherently ambiguous questions, such as: What is the best way to spend a day off? What is the optimal use of $10,000? What is the correct way to treat a depressed client? Personality dynamics and psychopathology are inherently ambiguous areas. Thus, the creation of a theory to which one remains loyal in the absence of objective evidence represents a fundamental error in clinical treatment. In this respect, the emphasis in this volume is on identifying relevant patterns rather than focusing on abstract issues, such as loss or abandonment, as a way to minimize the focus on unprovable projections. Are the patterns themselves projections? To some extent, they undoubtedly are. But the focus on structure is encouraged here as a way to *minimize* the projections of the "meaning" of the associated content.

Even the cognitive therapy model, because of its extensive consideration of cognitive distortions, is being attacked by critics who emphasize that equating psychological health with rationality results in a flawed equation (Safran & Segal, 1990; Guidano, 1987). Beyond this criticism of cognitive therapy, there is an important philosophical issue regarding the "reality" that is theoretically distorted and evident in the client's cognitive distortions. By viewing an individual's psychological problems as derived from errors in thinking, it is inevitable that the question will be raised, "Who is the authority on reality to be entrusted the determination of what constitutes a distortion?" Critics of the cognitive therapy model have not been satisfied with the way in which cognitive therapists have dealt with the issue of who has the final say on what reality is and is not. Cognitive therapists have generally responded that there is no ultimate authority on what is real and what is not, and that one can only consider the outcomes of a particular line of thinking, feeling, and behaving. There are those who will interpret this as an evasion of the responsibility to address the question definitively. Unfortunately, that conclusion presupposes that there is a definitive answer to the question. It should be readily apparent that there is not.

In recent years especially, the question of how reality is created has received considerable attention in the psychotherapy literature. The emergence of the great interest in brief therapy methods, in particular, has led to a careful examination of the question of how subjective realities are formed. Hypnosis has played a pivotal role in catalyzing this widespread interest in brief therapy approaches (Haley, 1973, 1982). Consider the extensive influence of Milton Erickson on the Mental Research Institute (MRI) group of Paul Watzlawick, Richard Fisch, Gregory Bateson, Jay Haley, John Weakland, and other short-term therapy catalysts (Watzlawick, 1982; Fisch, 1982; Weakland, 1982). Their powerful hypnotic and interactional viewpoints were able to emerge only when we redefined our perceptions of reality concerning the nature of therapeutic interaction. More recently, the emphasis has increased on developing an appreciation for the relevance of the constructivist viewpoint advocated by Paul Watzlawick and others (Watzlawick, 1984; Foerster, 1984). This perspective has at its core the belief that reality is shaped by what we say it is (Glaserfeld, 1984). To adopt such a view is to say that reality is malleable and subjective. Of course, at some level, anyone in clinical practice already has a fundamental belief that one's subjective experience can change. The recent emphasis on brief therapy has fostered a great deal of interest in developing active methodologies for bringing change about as quickly as possible.

Hypnosis is far more art than science. Trance states and hypnotic realities have yet to be measured in a definitive way, or to be defined with any precision. What makes it possible for a client to be in his or her "usual" frame of mind one moment and then deeply absorbed in an experience that precludes body awareness, as in hypnotic anesthesia, the next continues to elude complete understanding. The field of hypnosis responds to such highly subjective experiences with attempts to achieve some objective understanding of them, but the appreciation of subjective experience and of the value of phenomenology is ever present.

DISTINGUISHING BETWEEN THERAPEUTIC AND SYMPTOMATIC TRANCES

Recognizing hypnosis as a mechanism for creating subjective realities can help one appreciate the deeper implications of the previous statement that hypnosis is neither inherently good nor bad. Presented in this section are some characterizations of both therapeutic trances (i.e., those trance experiences that are deemed useful) and symptomatic trances (i.e., absorption in experiences that are considered dysfunctional or harmful).

Therapeutic Trances

Therapeutic trances may be temporary experiences of short duration, such as that found in a formal hypnosis session conducted by a therapist, or they may be the more extensive, individually generated viewpoints of self or life that are a by-product of socialization. Regardless of their content or duration, therapeutic trances are beneficial to the individual (Gilligan, 1987). In order for a trance to be considered therapeutic, it must have at least these characteristics:

1. It enhances the quality of the person's self-image and life experience.
2. It facilitates a meaningful and positive rapport between the individual and the significant others in this individual's life.
3. It manifests flexibility—the ability to adapt in a responsive and timely way to changing circumstances.
4. It is context appropriate, meaning that the portion of reality to which the individual responds fits in a beneficial way that is congruent with the individual's intentions and desires.
5. It enhances the individual's ability to recognize, accept, and effectively utilize the different parts of himself or herself.
6. It allows for positive possibilities that motivate the individual to act in a responsible and goal-directed manner.

The various components of therapeutic trances combine to permit growth and adaptation in a self-contained system that is able to generate positive and context-appropriate responses to various life experiences.

Symptomatic Trances

Clients' symptoms may be viewed as an unfortunate by-product of the same structures of hypnosis that might, in a different context, generate therapeutic effects. Daniel Araoz (1985) described what he called "negative self-hypnosis" in a similar vein when he considered how hypnosis can generate unwanted symptoms. The term "symptomatic trance" refers to the circumstance of an individual's having generated a view of self and life that leads to unwanted symptomatic experiences (Gilligan, 1987). The components of symptomatic trances include:

1. Self-limiting, self-destructive ways of responding to life experience.
2. Poor rapport with the significant others in one's life, creating the kinds of unsatisfying—even destructive—relationships commonly observed among depressed clients.

3. Perception of reality that is rigidly adhered to, despite over-whelming, even pain-inducing, evidence that directly suggests that the person's view is in dire need of modification, and in which the individual displays a markedly impaired ability to recognize and adapt to changing circumstances that would require generating novel or modified responses.
4. Behavioral responses that are context-inappropriate in that the individual does not recognize or respond meaningfully to the demand characteristics of the situations he or she faces, gen-erating the experiences that are then viewed as failure, rejec-tion, humiliation, and so forth.
5. Self-rejection that manifests an inability to accept and appro-priately utilize the different parts of oneself.

With regard to the last item, the client in a symptomatic trance creates a dysfunctional dissociation within himself or herself by labeling a part (or parts) of the self as negative and useless. In so doing, a dysfunctional dissociation is established that increases in direct proportion to the intensity of the attempts consciously made to "get rid of" such parts. Once a part of one's self has been labeled (e.g., "my terrible anger") and becomes the product of conscious but failing strategies of change, the gap between conscious and uncon-scious resources widens. This further promotes the likelihood that the dissociation will prove increasingly dysfunctional because of the polarity (rather than integration) that it fosters.

Context determines meaning

In contrasting therapeutic and symptomatic trances, the role of context is identified as a key component in differentiating the two types of trance experiences. All the various components of hypno-sis, from the classical hypnotic phenomena to the hypnotic aspects of social-influence communication, are equally evident in sympto-matic and therapeutic trances. The role of context is instrumental in helping to determine whether a particular hypnotic experience of focusing on a specific aspect of one's self (such as an expectation or a memory) is useful or not. Focusing one's attention on a partic-ular dimension of experience can be either helpful or hurtful, depending on how the focus is applied. What represents an asset in one context can be a liability in another. For example, what seems like admirable tenacity in one area may be viewed as obstinacy in another.

As obvious as this may seem, therapists tend to emphasize only the positive potentials of their techniques, apparently with little regard for what it is about an individual and about a particular context that might make such a technique not only inappropriate, but even hazardous. The indications for and contraindications to a given pattern can only be identified in relation to a specific individual client.

DEPRESSION AND SYMPTOMATIC TRANCES

In the description of the general characteristics of symptomatic trances, a number of criteria were delineated that can help the reader define ways in which hypnosis may prove to be antitherapeutic (just as therapy techniques themselves might be antitherapeutic). In this section, the characteristics of symptomatic trances are elaborated as they specifically relate to depressed individuals.

The first criterion of a symptomatic trance relates to the overall poor quality of life experience. An individual's general or specific outlook on or response to life experience can lead him or her into the experience of depression. Depression detracts from the quality of life in countless ways; it is a painful experience that takes the joy out of life and makes life, at times, seem not worth enduring. The person in the rigid depressive framework is fully absorbed experientially in a way of being that is responded to as though it were "real." The depressed individual has evolved a viewpoint of self and life that is subjective and virtually arbitrary. In response to the "Rorschach of life," the client generates projections that are hurtful to the self. Because it is "believed-in imagination," the client does not realize that his or her version of reality is not an uplifting reflection of the possibilities life has to offer.

The lack of rapport with significant others represents a second aspect of the depressive's symptomatic trance. The evidence of dysfunction in the depressed individual's important relationships is conclusive. The poor rapport with others is manifested in a variety of ways, including an impoverished ability to recognize the strengths and weaknesses of important others (arising from vague, global assessments and leading to extensive personal emotional investment in the most impossible relationships) and the lack of the communication skills necessary to define one's own and/or relate to others' ongoing experiences in positive and relationship-enhancing ways. The current data suggest that at least 50 percent of those who are clinically depressed are also suffering marital and family dysfunctions, and, that at least 50 percent of those suffering marital and family dysfunctions can also be identified as clinically depressed (Beach & Nelson, 1990). The absence of effective rapport-building skills with significant others leads to isolation, alienation, withdrawal, feelings of rejection, humiliation, and the other, similar relationship-based complaints typical of depressives.

Some clinicians advocate the notion of depression as a choice, even badgering their depressed clients with variations of the question, "Why do you choose to be depressed?" Depression is *not* a choice! In fact, depression may be more meaningfully viewed as the *lack* of perceived choice, and herein lies the third criterion of a symptomatic trance: the individual lacks the flexibility that having multiple choices to employ in a given context permits. The result is a depressogenic rigidity of responses to life experience. There are many causes for depression, but, in virtually every client I have ever treated, there were *experiential deficits* that were clearly related to the experience of depression. By experiential deficit, I mean that in the individual's construction of his or her subjective reality, there were certain skills and experiences that were encouraged via socialization, as well as specific skills and experiences that were directly and indirectly discouraged. This inappropriate use of, or lack of, specific skills placed the individual at risk for depression.

In many ways, it is the things that the person does not know how to do that eventually surface as depression. The (depressive) symptomatic trance involves the unconscious, nonvolitional generation of the symptomatic experiences (i.e., cognitive distortions, dysfunctional relationships, absence of problem-solving capabilities, rigid mind-sets) that are the appropriate targets for treatment. The nonvolitional, and hence dissociative, aspect of the symptomatic experience represents the third criterion of a symptomatic trance.

The notion of rigidity as a function of symptomatic trances is a concept that has many profound implications for the treatment process. Rigidity means an invariant response on the part of the client regardless of changing contexts. Whether one refers to it as a fixation or as a developmental arrest, a fixed behavioral, cognitive, or emotional response is precisely the mechanism whereby the person places himself or herself at odds with parts of the self or environment (Samko, 1986; Zeig, 1980a).

The writers on cognitive therapy expound extensively on the various methods designed to deal with the rigidity of the client's belief system and patterns of thinking. The interpersonal model focuses on the rigid and dysfunctional relationship patterns the individual employs, attempting to broaden, diversify, and establish some flexibility and the ability to relate to others in a more meaningful and satisfying way. Even psychodynamic approaches recognize the rigidity of the client's patterns for relating to self and others, exploring those rigidities in the context of a transference relationship with the therapist.

A distinguishing characteristic of the symptomatic trance in general, and the depressive trance in particular, is the invariant quality of the client's responses. The client attempts to do what he or she knows how to do based on preexisting, but maladaptive, patterns and is unable to shift strategies as necessary. Furthermore, the client does not distinguish between failed attempts and *being* a failure. A primary goal of any therapist who is working with a depressed client, regardless of his or her preferred theoretical orientation, is to help the client evolve a more flexible way for dealing with life experience by emphasizing the need continually to monitor and adapt to changing life circumstances. Simply put, the responses that were adequate before may not be adequate now, just as the responses that are adequate now may not be adequate later. (Even what appear to be solutions in therapy now can become problems later if flexibility is not actively taught.) Unless the client is instructed on how to maintain flexibility and continually adapt himself or herself to changing contexts, the clinician can unwittingly reinforce rigidity on the part of the client by encouraging the belief that there is one correct way of approaching some problem, when, in fact, there are many correct ways to do so.

The fourth component of symptomatic trances is a context-inappropriate response that indicates that the depressed individual is not employing the most useful dimension of experience—the best response—in reacting to a particular context. One of the goals of treatment, particularly in light of what has been said about rigidities, is to be able to generate the best response in a given context. Context-inappropriate responses mean that the person is relying on or accessing an inappropriate resource for the situation at hand. Furthermore, the individual is not adjusting his or her behavior, thoughts, or feelings to be congruent with the circumstances. For example, becoming absorbed in thoughts or feelings leading to a preoccupation with one's self (focusing internally) when meeting someone is a strategy for missing relevant details of the encounter, including such basic elements as the person's name (five minutes later, one has to ask, "I'm sorry, what was your name?"). Being focused internally in a situation that requires an external orientation is an example of a context-inappropriate focal point. Likewise, to be focused on one's feelings and needs to the exclusion of situational cues is what permits the comic scenario of a teenager smashing his parents' car and then, while his parents are vigorously communicating their displeasure, asking, "Does this mean that I won't be able to use the car on Friday night?"

Life presents an ongoing series of situations that must be perceived and responded to effectively if one is to minimize the stresses of daily life. Depressed individuals, because of their preoccupation with internal and unpleasant experience, often miss obvious opportunities to better their situation by generating inappropriate responses to the circumstances they confront. This understanding represents a fundamentally different view of depression than does framing depressives as "sick."

Symptomatic trances involve self-rejection, a fifth distinguishing criterion. Beck (1967) described as one aspect of his "negative triad of depression" the negative self-evaluation typical of depressives. In hypnotic terms, the individual is negatively dissociated, labeling specific parts of himself or herself as unacceptable or unworthy. Thus, people who are depressed present such common complaints as, "I need to get rid of my anger," or "I want you to help me get rid of my _____ (fill in the blank)." Self-rejection of inevitable parts of one's self is an unfortunate way of framing basic components of one's personality. How does one "get rid of" anger? How does one "get rid of" sexuality, or an appetite for sweets, or any other part of the self? It is unrealistic to believe that one can get rid of fundamental components of one's self. Thus, by operating according to the erroneous idea that it is possible to do so, the client may repeatedly attempt to "get rid of" such basic components of himself or herself and naturally fail, reinforcing the perception that he or she is a victim.

From a hypnotic standpoint, any time someone identifies a part, labels that part, and gives it a force and personality all its own, he or she is effectively employing a mechanism of dissociation. When an individual creates such dissociations within himself or herself, these parts do not have any positive associations, or triggers, to ways in which they might be beneficially applied. Dissociation, like all classical trance phenomena, has the potential to be either helpful or hurtful, depending on how it is applied. The self-rejection of devalued parts establishes an antitherapeutic dissociation that precludes the client's developing an appreciation for the potential value of any given part while learning how to apply it appropriately in a given context.

This kind of dissociation has always plagued the hypnosis field, but it is particularly apparent when considering the use of hypnosis in treating depression. Some influential people decades ago, most notably Freud, employed a form of hypnosis in such a way that it generated undesirable consequences. They erroneously concluded that hypnosis was not useful for depression. As a result, hypnosis became dissociated from the treatment of depression over the following years, and instead of clinicians learning how to use the tool properly, hypnosis maintained its dysfunctionally dissociated position. This scenario is structurally identical to that in which a client labels anger "bad" and tries to get rid of it, instead of learning to apply it skillfully in an appropriate context.

How does one evolve the self-rejecting perspective evident in symptomatic trances? It may come from the injunctions embedded in the communications of significant others that suggest (directly or indirectly) that this part is not valued in relation to them. Or it may be a part that was context inappropriate at some point in this individual's life and he or she overgeneralized beyond the specific context that this part was wholly "bad."

The sixth and final aspect of symptomatic trances is the client's use of the trance to amplify negative focal points or negative expectations through imagery and other hypnotic patterns. Of course, the client does this unintentionally. As a direct consequence of being absorbed in the "believed-in imagination" of his or her world view, the person does not consciously recognize that he or she is selectively attending to negative focal points or generating negative imagery. Clearly, however, the attentiveness to and absorption in the negative aspects of experience represent one of the great challenges of working therapeutically—and especially hypnotic—with the depressed client. Very often, therapeutic strategy simply involves changing the content of these negative focal points and images. It is as if the hypnotist/clinician is simply saying, "Focusing on these thoughts, feelings and images is hurting you; focus on these *other* thoughts, feelings, and images instead, you'll feel better."

The selective attention to negativity inevitably magnifies it, thereby diminishing any awareness of the positive portion of experience, and thus fueling ongoing depressive experience. It is noteworthy that the clinician can also focus the client, intentionally or otherwise, on negative focal points. For example, the conventional wisdom of psychotherapy has been that focusing the client on his or her anger would encourage ventilation and redirect the hypothetical "anger turned inward" popularly viewed by Freud as the underlying mechanism of depression. Many years and many studies later, we now know that focusing people on anger helps to make them angry, but it does not improve their experience of depression in any significant way (Tavris, 1989). To focus someone on a minimally relevant dimension of the depressive experience is a guaranteed mechanism for encouraging a lengthy, time-consuming, emotionally charged, but therapeutically ineffective, treatment.

The client's focal points in imagery are hypnotic amplifications of portions of experience. To be therapeutic, the amplified experiences and their associations must be relevant and useful. The use of inappropriate focal points or inappropriate imagery can have potentially disastrous consequences for the client. This point in particular highlights why depression has been considered a disorder that should not be treated hypnotically. Hypnosis amplifies experience. If the clinician uses hypnosis to amplify feelings of anger, hopelessness, or victimization, then it is predictable that the client's condition will deteriorate. On the other hand, hypnosis can be skillfully used to amplify hopefulness, problem-solving capabilities, and other abilities helpful in both the recovery from depression and the prevention of future relapses. While the depressed client uses trance symptomatically to focus on dimensions of experience that are hurtful, the clinician's tasks are to interrupt that symptomatic trance, build a therapeutic one that amplifies salient and positive portions of experience, and make these new associations available to the client to access in an autonomous manner.

It should now be apparent to the reader how hypnosis can be applied in antitherapeutic ways. By identifying some of the common denominators associated with symptomatic trances, it is suggested that hypnosis can be employed skillfully, permitting one to avoid the hazards associated with unwittingly reinforcing the symptomatic aspects of the client's depressive trance state.

TRANCE PHENOMENA EVIDENT IN DEPRESSIVE SYMPTOM PHENOMENA

This section describes how the classical hypnotic phenomena, which may be viewed as mechanisms for creating subjective experience, are typically utilized in the depressive client. The classical hypnotic phenomena outlined in the following list are best thought of as building blocks of experience—both positive and negative (Yapko, 1990).

TABLE 2. CLASSICAL HYPNOTIC PHENOMENA

- Age regression (including hypermnesia and revivification)
- Age progression
- Amnesia
- Analgesia
- Anesthesia
- Catalepsy
- Dissociation
- Hallucinations (positive and negative)
- Ideodynamic responses
- Sensory alteration
- Time distortion

The classical hypnotic phenomena delineated are, in various combinations, the identifiable structures in *all* experiences. The next list outlines how the various trance phenomena typically surface in the experience of depression.

TABLE 3. HYPNOTIC PHENOMENA EVIDENT IN DEPRESSION

- Age regression (including hypermnesia and revivification)
    Primarily past focus
    Recalling/reexperiencing past hurts, rejections, humiliations, etc.
    Using the past as the reference for life decisions
- Age Progression
    Projecting past hurts into future contexts
- Amnesia
    Lack of conscious recall of past successes or positive feedback
- Catalepsy
    Psychomotor retardation and rigid posturing
- Dissociation
    Depressive affect independent of context
    Selective attention paid to negatives
    Dissociation from present context in favor of past orientation
    Self-labeling "parts" negatively (e.g., anger)
- Ideodynamic responses
    Automatic depressogenic thoughts, feelings, sensations, behaviors
- Hallucinations
    Perceived rejection and negativity where none are present
    Inability to see or hear positive feedback
- Sensory alteration
    Altered relationship to one's body via physiological symptoms (e.g., somatization)
    Diminished sensory awareness and sensory enjoyment
- Time distortion
    Extended experience of past and current discomfort
    Diminished experience of future possibilities

Viewing various aspects of depressive experience in terms of classical hypnotic phenomena provides a different framework for conceptualizing and implementing interventions. In this section, I elaborate on how each of these trance phenomena relates to the overall depressive experience.

Age Regression (Including Hypermnesia and Revivification)

Depressives typically manifest an extraordinary preoccupation with their past. They often dwell on details of past hurts so much that if they think about the future at all, it is in a very limited way that invariably has its roots in the past. Statements such as, "I will never have a good relationship because I never had one" reflect the preoccupation with the past and its use as the reference point for predicting the future. The underlying message is, "I will not ever be happy until my parents treat me better when I was a child!"

The paralyzing preoccupation with the past is a primary component of the depression's structure. Therefore, for a clinician to use exclusively past-oriented approaches in therapy reinforces the client's dysfunctional preoccupation with the past instead of working to establish a better future.

Age Progression

In the previous section, I described how the typical depressive is focused on past hurts. The client has very little positive expectation for the future. It is typical for the client to relate to the future only in a limited way, simply superimposing present and past hurts onto the future, as if the future could only hold more of the same. In the extreme, this perspective may be so overwhelming that suicide begins to seem like a reasonable alternative. In the absence of a realistic orientation to the future, age progression techniques are integral to effective treatment.

Amnesia

States of intense subjective distress impair a person's attentional focus and, as a result, his or her ability to recall. Memory requires a considerable degree of continuity of experience. Often, a deeply distressed client will jump from thought to thought, from moment to moment, with very little continuity. This same structure of jumping from thought to thought with little apparent connection between them is precisely how amnesia may be deliberately facilitated hypnotically in structured amnesia techniques (Lankton & Lankton, 1983; Zeig, 1985). The depressed individual experiences a continuous flow of negativity, which is (spontaneously) generated through his or her thoughts, feelings, and actions. Consequently, there is a discontinuity about positive experiences, which creates a climate for amnesia about successes or episodes of positive feedback. Positives are so disconnected from ongoing (negative) experience as to be easily discounted and, consequently, forgotten.

Catalepsy

One of the classic symptoms of depression described in the DSM-III-R (APA, 1987) is psychomotor retardation. In hypnotic terms, the intense attentional absorption of being in a symptomatic (depressive) trance gives rise to the hypnotic phenomenon of catalepsy. Catalepsy is technically defined as the inhibition of voluntary movement (Erickson & Rossi, 1979, 1981), and it is considered to be a predictable manifestation of a client who is deeply absorbed in the experience of hypnosis. The cataleptic response of the formally hypnotized client and the catalepsy of the individual deeply absorbed in depressive experience are similar.

Dissociation

The role of dissociation in symptomatic experiences is increasingly recognized as substantial. It is prevalent in disorders such as post-traumatic stress disorder and anxiety disorders, and it is, not surprisingly, the primary distinguishing feature of what are known as the dissociative disorders. Dissociation also plays a significant role in depression. First, as I have already described, a person will so intently focus on internal experiences that he or she effectively dissociates from the context at hand. Second, there is also an element of dissociation present in the selective attention of focusing on negatives to the exclusion of positives. Everyone has both positive and negative experiences, but for the depressive, positive experiences may be dissociated from awareness, leaving only the negative portion of the experiential continuum. Third, there is a temporal dissociation that takes place as the client withdraws from the immediacy of his or her life contexts, while gradually becoming more immersed in the pain and memories of past experience. Fourth, labeling parts of oneself negatively fuels a dysfunctional dissociation to those parts. This is done by establishing only negative associations to that part, and by not establishing any positive triggers to a context in which that particular part can be usefully (and even favorably) expressed. There is a maxim in the psychotherapy world that states that "the more you try to control a part of yourself, the more that part controls you." In the case of depression, where the person negatively evaluates himself or herself on a continuous basis, the parts of the self are dissociated. None of the parts seems valuable anywhere, which fuels the poor self-esteem characteristic of depression.

Ideodynamic Responses

Ideodynamic responses reflect the "automatic" (i.e., unconscious) sensations, thoughts, feelings, perceptions, and behaviors that are associated with ongoing experience. Since experience coexists in multiple dimensions at all times, whenever experience is generated in one dimension, the unconscious (automatic) associations are inevitably triggered in other dimensions. Thus, as one thinks about suggestions that are offered, one experiences the associations related to that information, including sensory, emotional, and motoric. In the case of depression, Beck (Beck et al., 1979; Beck, 1987) has described in detail the role of automatic thoughts and automatic feelings typical of the depressive. His strategy is to interrupt their automatic nature through consciously identifying and then deliberately refuting them. As automatic, unconscious aspects of experience, they may be considered ideodynamic responses.

Hallucinations

Hypnotic hallucinations describe the relationship between sensory experiences and external realities. A positive hallucination involves having a sensory experience that has no external cause. A negative hallucination is evident when a person does not have a sensory experience despite the presence of a sensory stimulus. The depressive has the ability to perceive rejection and negativity where, in fact, none is present. The individual projects, on a positive hallucinatory basis, the negative responses of the environment and is not responding to the objective cues available there.

Similarly, the fact that a client is unable to see (hear or feel) the kinds of positive feedback that his or her life experience objectively provides can be thought of as a series of negative hallucinations in the various sensory modalities. When the client negatively hallucinates positive feedback—success in handling situations, compliments from peers, or other positive forms of feedback—it is easy to appreciate how negative hallucinations can fuel the amnesia that leads the person to disconnect these experiences from his or her awareness and relegate them to an insignificant position in his or her life.

Sensory Alteration

Sensory alteration is the ability of the hypnotized individual to alter various sensory cues in order to experience himself or herself differently. Sensory experiences in any of the sensory modalities can be enhanced or diminished, depending on how the hypnotic process is structured. In the case of the depressed client, the individual generally diminishes his or her sensory capabilities. It is not atypical for such a client, while in a depressive episode, to view life as colorless— food is bland, sensory experience is dull, sexuality is absent (or nearly so). In general, sensory experience is markedly diminished so that a previously colorful life becomes depressingly gray and dismal.

A sensory alteration also becomes evident as the client manifests depressive experience through physiological symptoms. It is common for depressives to report vague somatic complaints. Pleasurable sensory stimuli are diminished in the person's awareness, and unpleasant stimuli are amplified. These represent fundamental sensory alterations within the symptomatic trance.

Time Distortion

For the depressed individual, time can lose all objective measure. Implicit in the statement that "time flies when you're having fun" is that time lags when you are having a bad time. Depression is an ongoing bad time. Consequently, it is typical for the depressive to feel

like every minute of every hour of every day is endless in its unpleas-
antness. Time distortion also means that a bad moment or bad morning, instead of being realistically confined to a limited time span,
becomes extended to a bad day, and a bad day becomes a bad week,
and a bad week becomes a bad month. Finally, time distortion is evident in the extended experience of past and current discomfort and
in the diminished experience of positive future possibilities.

THE BUILDING BLOCKS OF DEPRESSION

The classical trance phenomena, as the building blocks of experience, can be readily identified in the depressed client's experience.
Fundamental to effective hypnotic strategy planning is the recognition that it is not therapeutic simply to immerse the person in more
of the hypnotic experience that he or she already is generating. Therapeutic hypnotic experience reinforces for the person components
that are complementary to the core aspects of the symptomatic
trance experience. In other words, hypnosis is best applied by structuring experiences for the depressed client that lie beyond the
boundaries of his or her symptomatic trance. For example, if the
depressed client is unusually focused on past hurts and failures, it
is up to the clinician to structure hypnotic experiences and associations of positive future possibilities as a way of going beyond the
parameters of the client's self-generated symptomatic trance.

IMPLICATIONS OF THE HYPNOTIC FRAMEWORK

By adopting a view of depression as a consequence of a symptomatic
trance (i.e., the client's misapplication of trance phenomena), the clinician is in a better position to appreciate the phenomenology of the
client's depression. One of the reasons that depression takes so many
different forms—complicating the search for standardized and universal diagnostic criteria—is that hypnotic experience itself is so
extraordinarily subjective and variable a process. In this respect, it
is easy to appreciate how those therapies that have most reliably
proved effective in the treatment of depression can achieve the positive results they do. Specifically, cognitive, interpersonal, and

problem-solving therapies work so well because they provide experiences complementary to the structures of the symptomatic trance the client is in. For example, when the client is too focused internally on his or her feelings, these therapeutic modalities include a directive to the client to focus on thoughts and to test reality through external feedback. With such a complement, it is no wonder that clients in these treatment modalities tend to improve so rapidly. Contrast such approaches with the psychodynamic approaches, which, instead of teaching the client to focus on a concrete and definable set of problems, encourage the already confused client to become even more abstract and diffuse by focusing on nebulous, poorly defined issues. When the client shows, as a basic part of the problem, a dysfunctional preoccupation with the past, greater emphasis on the past does not teach the kind of complementary skills the depressed client needs.

The hypnotic framework for understanding depression also carries with it an implicit explanation for some aspects of the biological correlates of depression. Anyone who is well versed in hypnosis understands the powerful relationship between mind and body. Even though this relationship has not yet been defined in any substantive way, it is obvious from even the simplest performance of a relaxation process that mental processes influence the body's experience.

Viewing depression as involving a symptomatic trance acknowledges the need to provide direction to the client, even if only indirectly. If the depressed client knew how to do what needed to be done in order to improve, he or she would surely have done it. The antitherapeutic application of self-hypnosis in creating a dysfunctional subjective reality causes the most suffering of all. The client does not recognize his or her existing (but unconscious) patterns and their inherent limitations when he or she comes in for treatment. It is the clinician's job to identify and expand upon those patterns in order to permit greater adaptability and flexibility in responding to life's demands. The clinician is the active agent of change in the utilization framework.

Working effectively in a utilization framework precludes the use of standardized approaches. One of the greatest setbacks to the field of clinical hypnosis has been the overemphasis on trance as a fixed capability existing solely within the client. This emphasis allowed practitioners to maintain the illusion that an individual either does or does not have the capacity for trance. Thus, technique became less important than ritual, and relationship became less important than individual susceptibility. The utilization approach stresses the need to individualize approaches according to individual clients.

With the standardization of approaches, any real contact with the idiosyncratic nature of the client's world is impossible. Essentially, fixed treatment approaches imply that all depressed clients are alike—an assumption that is fundamentally false. The hypnotic framework is most powerful for relating to (accepting and utilizing) the individual client's world. Given that depression has multiple causes, its treatment must also be multifaceted.

Hypnosis emphasizes the phenomenology of all experience. Employing the hypnotic framework for understanding and relating to the depressed client's world opens up countless possibilities for intervention that are not available in more theory-specific approaches. The balance of this book explores a variety of ways for employing hypnosis with the goal of shifting the client's symptomatic trance experience of life to a therapeutic one.

6

Stages of Treatment

The hypnotic framework can provide valuable insights into the structure of the client's inner associations that serve to create and maintain depression. In the previous chapter, emphasis was placed on the notion of trance as a neutral phenomenon, capable of generating both symptomatic and therapeutic results. The structures of experience are parallel in symptomatic and therapeutic trances, but they vary in content, intensity, sequence, and other salient characteristics. For example, a client may visualize either being rejected in an upcoming interaction or getting approved. Although the content changes (rejection or approval), the structure of the expectation is constant; namely, the use of visual imagery involving social interaction.

Having described some of the components of depression from a hypnotic standpoint, this chapter considers the structure of hypnotically based treatment from within a utilization framework. The model presented may be viewed as a generic theoretical model of intervention, one that is entirely compatible with but independent of a specific therapy model (such as cognitive or interpersonal). This model is based on the concept of stages of treatment that can be viewed as the fundamental patterns (structures) of psychotherapy with depressed clients, regardless of one's preferred theoretical framework and style of intervention.

By analyzing the considerable number of successful cases reported by leading practitioners, as well as keeping detailed descriptions of my own depressed clients' progress and my methods of intervention, I have identified these stages of treatment as integral to successful intervention. Various clinicians may spend more or less time at a particular stage, or may alter the sequence; however, in order for a clinician to intervene successfully in the treatment of a depressed individual, these stages of treatment should be considered for their relevance.

The following list outlines the various stages of treatment I have conceptualized.

TABLE 4. STAGES OF TREATMENT

- Interview and information gathering
- Building expectancy
- Facilitating flexibility
- Expanding perceptual frames of reference
- Experimenting with choices
- Solidifying situational specificity
- Integration of feedback mechanisms regarding:
    Situational demands
    Influence of previous patterns on perceived choices
    Relative rigidity or flexibility of responses
    Satisfactory level of responses
    Need for more information or alternatives
- Incorporation
- Limits of generalizations (future orientation)

These stages are described in detail in the following, along with the specific goals of treatment at each stage and the role that hypnosis can play in shaping the success of that stage and facilitating the overall progress of the therapy.

STAGES OF TREATMENT

Interview and Information Gathering

The manner in which the interview is conducted plays a huge role in shaping the style and quality of interaction between therapist and client, and thus it dictates to a large extent what will be possible in the therapy. In the first session, there are a number of specific goals to be achieved: (1) identifying the salient issues (i.e., content) that are immediately related to the client's depressed condition; (2) identifying the associated ongoing patterns (i.e., structure) used by the client in the past and likely to be used again for organizing perceptions and responding to life experiences (detailed in *When Living Hurts*, Yapko, 1988); (3) identifying specific client resources from which the treatment process can draw and those resources that will need to be established in order for the person to recover; (4) identifying through the use of "how" questions (e.g., " How do you know when it's safe to self-disclose?") the strategy the person uses to form perceptions and make decisions, in order to identify what is incorrect, irrelevant, or missing; and (5) establishing an attitude and demeanor that encourage the therapeutic relationship to be defined as a collaborative one. Additional important factors to consider at the beginning of the treatment process are noted in the following list.

TABLE 5. BEGINNING THERAPY

- Establish expectations, goals
    Structure, content, clarity, and feasibility of goals
- Build rapport, establish feedback patterns
- Establish timing for the unfolding of the therapy
- Assess:
    Suicide potential
    Current level of discomfort
    Degree of pervasiveness of symptomatic patterns
    Central, peripheral depressive patterns
    Degree of balance of subjective patterns
    Range and quality of personal resources to access and
        contextualize
    Level and quality of responsiveness to clinician
- Assess immediacy of the need for symptom relief via hypnosis
- Establish a context for the therapy's succeeding ("expectancy")

Identifying key life issues and the characteristic patterns with which the person responds to those issues is necessary in order to identify appropriate targets for intervention. From the outset, the clinician needs to highlight the importance of the client's actively learning new ways of organizing internal experience and external behaviors.

Hypnosis can be introduced in the first session as a core component of the overall treatment plan. Hypnosis can be used diagnostically and therapeutically, and the client can be instructed as to the role it plays in shaping one's perceptions and sense of subjective reality. The client can be taught to think about reality as a subjectively conceived and maintained state of existence, meaning, in part, that the same patterns that might have generated symptomatic consequences can now be used differently for therapeutic purposes.

As the clinician seeks descriptions of the phenomenological experience of the client, the opportunities for recognizing trance phenomena in the depressed client's "symptomatic trance" are substantial. Furthermore, when describing the experience of depression, the client is likely to provide the clinician with personal imagery that can be incorporated into the treatment plan. For example, therapeutic hypnotic processes are indirectly suggested to the clinician when a client describes his or her depression as a "dark cloud hanging over my head," or as "dragging around a heavy ball and chain all the time." The client's description of the depression can often yield ideas for therapeutic imagery that can be used to shift the way the client represents his or her experience, transforming it in quality and intensity.

An important goal of the interview and information-gathering phase is to obtain clear, detailed descriptions from the client about his or her experience of the depression in order to become familiar with the kind of language the client uses. The client's spontaneous description of experience is invariably the most revealing about how he or she organizes internal experience. The identification of salient patterns in the client's experience can be accomplished through careful consideration of the client's word choices and the patterns such choices reflect (such as cognitive style, response style, primary representational system, and the other patterns described in *When Living Hurts*).

The importance of establishing in the very first session that the relationship between clinician and client is a collaborative one cannot be overstated. A popular misconception is that the clinician who employs hypnosis has a rigid expectation of communicating specific information or demands with which the client must comply. The utilization approach requires the therapist to be highly client-centered in identifying, accepting, and employing existing client patterns in the service of the therapy. Because depressed clients tend to already feel victimized and helpless, anything but a collaborative approach simply reinforces one of the most dysfunctional aspects of the client's depression. The authoritarian style of the traditional hypnotherapist, and not hypnosis per se, is part of what made hypnosis untenable in the past.

Building Expectancy

The recognition that the depressed client holds negative expectations about the future is well documented in the clinical literature. It is vital to the treatment process to impart to the depressed client, in as many ways as possible, the notion that the future holds a realistic promise of change. Even when the client is trapped in unchangeable circumstances (debilitating illness, for example), the client's orientation toward the future must be addressed in such a way that the client can attain some level of hopefulness that will motivate participation in the treatment.

Having positive expectations for its success is generally considered an important ingredient of therapy. However, few models of treatment give more than cursory attention to *how* to establish positive expectations. In the treatment of depressed individuals in particular, the need to pay deliberate and focused attention to the issue of expectancy is probably the greatest factor in determining whether the therapy will ultimately prove beneficial. The reasons for this are described in detail in the next chapter, but for now, suffice it to say that the most essential aspect of treatment, the base upon which everything else in therapy is built, is the realm of expectancy. If the clinician does not understand the value of evolving positive expectations within the treatment, the likelihood of obtaining successful long-term therapeutic results is greatly diminished.

Expectancy may be positive or negative. Positive expectancy is the belief that the future holds promise for changing life conditions. The hopelessness that is characteristic of the depressive is a powerful reflection of a negative expectancy that the quality of life will (continue to) deteriorate, and of a lack of belief in a future that can, in some significant way, be better than the painful present or past.

It is no coincidence that when therapy is successful, the stage of building expectancy was the first intervention phase. Without positive expectations—the essence of hopefulness—there is no reason for the client to participate meaningfully in treatment.

Facilitating Flexibility

The rigidity of the depressed client's beliefs, values, and style of responding to life experience is well known. It is a goal of this stage of treatment that the client learn to recognize that the rigid manner in which he or she applies ineffective, even dysfunctional, patterns in responding to life experience is at the heart of his or her depression. "Rigidity" refers to the application of a specific pattern in a context where it is not only inappropriate, but even destructive. The philosophy behind the methods described in this book shifts the focus away from the notion of the depressed individual as "pathological," and instead recognizes that the client is symptomatic on the basis of inadequate skills and a restricted range of responses in a given context. The client is simply operating on the basis of subjective patterns, including subjective interpretations of reality, that are ineffective for meeting life demands.

Why does the client rigidly maintain dysfunctional patterns? Simply put, the client does so because of the lack of any other perceived choices. Part of the depressed client's problem (symptomatic trance) is the belief that the applied patterns *can* and *should* work in meeting the demands posed. Typically, the client's patterns did work at some point. However, when circumstances changed, the person's responses did not. The goal, then, of this particular stage of treatment is to facilitate flexibility in place of rigidity.

The individual's symptoms may be viewed as a product of rigidity; symptoms will remit when he or she has evolved other ways to respond to life experience that are more satisfying (i.e., immediate and effective) in terms of meeting life's demands and producing more desirable outcomes. In facilitating flexibility, emphasis is placed on communicating to the client that (1) there is a variety of valid viewpoints for interpreting life experiences, (2) it is necessary to evolve a variety of problem-solving skills, and (3) the client must be responsive to externals and how they relate to internal experiences. In this respect, a goal of the clinician is to communicate that there are many right ways to accomplish a goal, showing the client that if one attempts to do something and fails, one can use another approach.

This represents a powerful reframing that emphasizes that the client is not a failure; but rather, that the client's method (strategy) for addressing the given concern is ineffective.

Furthermore, by focusing on strategies, the clinician models responsiveness to the most important goal-defining question: "Familiarity aside, what is the best response one can generate in the particular context of concern?" By encouraging the client to think in terms of identifying the best response—realistic and appropriate—in a given context, instead of only focusing on feelings, the clinician is beginning to teach the necessary skill of compartmentalization. This can help the client make the distinction between internal feelings and external realities, which is very important as much of what depression is about is the client's inability to make such a distinction with any degree of precision.

The phase of facilitating flexibility in treatment is a deliberate attempt on the part of the clinician to continually communicate to the client that much of life experience is inherently ambiguous and that there are various ways to manage one's life successfully. This represents a significant shift for the client, who has only known one way (as a result of dichotomous thinking) to approach things—a way that has not worked. The pragmatic emphasis on doing things that work is a significant learning for the depressive, requiring attentiveness to detail and the defining of things in concrete terms, thereby increasing the likelihood of responding to situations with relevant information and a detailed consideration of what the situation requires as an effective response.

Expanding Frames of Reference

Closely related to the notion of rigidity as a primary structural element of depression is the notion that a necessary goal of treatment is to help the client expand his or her frames of reference. It was described earlier how it is characteristically human to interpret life experience on the basis of one's own frame of reference. Realistically, how could one do otherwise?

When one has as a frame of reference a flexible and broad range of personal experiences and skills upon which to draw for problem solving, rigidity is markedly diminished. But if the client's range of experience is narrow, or the client's problem-solving capabilities are poor (in general or relative to the issues at hand), it is vital that the clinician provide new choices (i.e., new ways of thinking, feeling, and behaving) that will prove useful. New choices might include acquiring the new relationship skills that the interpersonal psychotherapy model would suggest, or learning to think more objectively as the cognitive therapy model would suggest, or learning to recognize and utilize personal resources more skillfully as the utilization model would suggest.

The common denominator of all these approaches is to impart to the client in as powerful a way as possible that there are other ways of responding to troublesome life experiences. Thus, in characterizing this important stage of treatment as one involving expanding frames of reference, I mean to imply that a teaching of alternative viewpoints and responses is integral to the successful treatment of depression.

A point of distinction between the methods advocated in this book and some of the more psychodynamically oriented approaches can be made regarding this particular stage of treatment. Specifically, emphasis is placed here on the necessity to teach, in the context of a collaborative relationship, other ways of responding to troublesome life circumstances. This approach places little or no emphasis on identifying why the individual's previous patterns have been unsuccessful. It is understood that the patterns did not serve well in specific important contexts. But little value is accorded "psychological archeology" in seeking an answer to the question of why the person was so poorly prepared to handle particular situations. This viewpoint is only possible when one begins to turn away from abstract dynamic issues and search for causal explanations (as if there were any) in response to the question "why," and instead directs attention to identifying disruptive patterns and looking for solutions.

The stage of expanding frames of reference represents the bulk of therapy, as the work of most therapy sessions is discovering alternative ways of responding effectively to ongoing life experience. Thus, it is in this stage of treatment that the clinician is most likely to employ hypnosis, in an effort to encourage alternative viewpoints and representations of experience. Furthermore, it is at this stage that the clinician is most likely to make use of directives, such as task assignments and behavioral experiments. It is up to the clinician to structure opportunities (such as those presented in *When Living*

Hurts) for the client to learn that other ways to solve problems and respond to life can be more successful than whatever he or she did previously. The directives the clinician employs can have a profound effect on the client as he or she realizes that the problem is not the client him- or herself, rather it is his or her way of doing things that is ineffective. This realization enhances self-esteem considerably as the client comes to recognize that he or she is not entirely dysfunctional by nature, but is ineffective in particular contexts. The client can then learn to continually seek more information and more alternatives to enable a more flexible response to life.

Experimenting with Choices

Moving the client from the phase of simply considering expanding frames of reference to actually experimenting with new choices is the goal of this stage of treatment. Although one might know abstractly that a different viewpoint or manner of responding to some life situation might prove beneficial, there is nothing so satisfying as *initiating action* on the basis of a new perspective or behavioral strategy and thereby accomplishing some desired goal.

The emphasis throughout this book is on experiential learning. One of the great values of hypnosis in this respect is that the clinician models, through the use of hypnosis, a willingness to experiment, to step outside one's usual parameters. Hypnosis encourages experimentation with the limits of one's perceptions; the directive practitioner utilizes this framework for all actions, in the belief that arbitrary assumptions must be challenged, new behaviors must be tried, and arbitrary and self-limiting perspectives must be challenged and overcome. These are the reasons why this stage of treatment moves the client powerfully in the direction of developing a way of being that involves greater flexibility and better problem-solving skills, for both current problems and those that might arise in the future.

It is the clinician's responsibility to create (at most) or co-create (at least) the kinds of structured learning opportunities that will yield successful results. The clinician wants to encourage and motivate the client, and so one task is to inspire in the client *some* ability to predict likely outcomes, including when one can safely anticipate success in an endeavor. The clinician must protect the client and *never* set him or her up to be hurt. One's directives may not always be immediately beneficial, but a fundamental principle of the mental health profession is to cause no harm. Thus, if a clinician encourages the client to experiment with new choices and new ways of handling life circumstances, it must be with the proper protection that assures the client of a positive outcome. (This will be discussed further in Chapter 9.)

Experimentation plays a powerful role in validating or invalidating one's perceptions, which is why it is important to have an outcome orientation in structuring treatment and encouraging the client. The following table lists some of the important dimensions of an outcome orientation in treatment.

TABLE 6. DIMENSIONS OF AN OUTCOME ORIENTATION

- Goals are described in concrete and positive terms
- Objective results are demonstrable
- Relates appropriately to a specific context
- Initiated either externally by the therapist or internally by the client, but is maintained by the client as a new situational choice
- Allows selectivity and flexibility in adapting to experience

---

In the same way that I would encourage clinicians to describe their goals in concrete and positive terms and to define how they would know when success is resulting, I would also want the client to be able to make good choices that relate appropriately to the specific contexts of his or her life. In that respect, the clinician may initially encourage the client to experiment with some new external behavior or internal response. The direction, therefore, initially comes from the clinician. However, it is like teaching anyone a new skill. First, you provide direction and support; when the individual knows how to do those things for himself or herself, guidance is no longer necessary. Although the therapeutic relationship is defined as a collaborative one, the goal is the client's eventual full independence from the clinician. When the client learns the value of experimentation and adaptation in life, his or her sense of autonomy increases dramatically. The client comes to recognize through experimentation that the clinician doesn't have all the answers, but is able to teach how to approach situations flexibly and with a willingness to experiment with different behaviors and attitudes.

Solidifying Situational Specificity

Situational specificity is a term that reflects the fact that much of what dictates one's response in a given situation is the demand characteristics of that situation. In essence, situational specificity refers to the fact that a person's preexisting personality traits can be suppressed in a particular situation in answer to the demands of the situation. In terms of treating depression, the marked internal absorption so characteristic of depressives typically leads the depressed client to miss situational demands (external cues) that indicate appropriate responses in a given situation. A goal of treatment is to learn to think clearly and realistically about life experience and life situations in order to be able to generate appropriate and effective responses. The stage of solidifying situational specificity thus refers to the need to help the client recognize what the demand characteristics of a situation are, especially as they relate to one's personal beliefs, values, attitudes, and other precursors to behavior.

For example, think of a personal trait that you would consider to be a stable and enduring characteristic. Could someone create a situation in which that trait would be unable to surface or would be overwhelmed by some competing trait or characteristic? The abundance of literature on that topic in the field of social psychology strongly suggests that the answer is Yes. Honest people in some circumstances may behave dishonestly. Peaceful people can be in circumstances where they react violently. In certain situations, sensitive people can react insensitively. In the treatment process, we want to communicate to our clients that they must respond realistically to the ongoing demands of life. Thus, it is of great importance that the individual learn to recognize how seemingly similar situations are different—how a particular context is different from any other context.

While it may seem obvious that the various situations we face differ in some way, this fact is often overlooked in clinical practice. Clinicians who routinely link responses in the here and now to responses of the past may unwittingly encourage the collapse of the boundaries between "then" and "now," which may move the client to respond dysfunctionally to "now" as if it were "then."

Often, it is the client who has removed the boundaries between "then" and "now" as a part of his or her symptomatic pattern. It is typical of the depressive to respond to what has been and not to what is, and the clinician should not reinforce this pattern by linking then and now. Even an idea as basic as classical "transference" is potentially destructive in the treatment of depressives. To encourage a depressed person, actively or passively, to respond to the clinician in the same way that he or she would respond to other authority figures is a disservice to the client. Encouraging the client to respond to someone new as if he or she were someone of historical importance strengthens the inability to make clear distinctions between situational demands and personal desires and feelings. This is generally an ineffective strategy of the depressive and needs to be corrected, not unintentionally reinforced.

From a treatment standpoint situational specificity involves creating circumstances *actively* and *deliberately* that will interrupt an existing pattern of the client's while encouraging the person to develop a new pattern. This idea is discussed at greater length in Chapter 9.

Integration of Feedback

Because of the marked internal absorption of the typical depressive, he or she misses opportunities to receive meaningful feedback from the environment. A necessary goal of treatment, then, is to teach the client to recognize how external circumstances (e.g., people's personalities, organizations) are structured so that the client will be able to relate to them in a positive way. If one considers some of the issues that depressed clients most commonly present, one can readily appreciate how the lack of recognition of relevant situational variables can put one at risk for depression. For example, an urgent desire for affection from someone who has great difficulty in expressing affection is a gross mismatch between one's internal needs and the external realities. Wanting approval, validation, support, recognition, love, respect, or anything else from others is usually not the problem. The problem is in the lack of recognition that a particular individual is unable or unwilling to respond accordingly. Thus, recognizing the value of feedback and the need to adjust oneself flexibly to the feedback of a given situation is a necessary skill to be taught at this stage of the treatment process.

Obtaining feedback and responding realistically to it depends on the following factors.

1. *The recognition of situational demands.* Each individual, in order to be functional, must recognize what an appropriate response is in a particular context. For example, a person who self-discloses sensitive information of a personal nature to a new acquaintance at a cocktail party is engaging in a risky, and even inappropriate, self-disclosure. If a client receives negative feedback, in the form of only polite interest or even outright rejection, that client may conclude that he or she is simply no good, instead of recognizing that the self-disclosure was inappropriate in that particular context.

2. *The influence of previous patterns on perceived choices.* An individual must learn to recognize how similar to or different from previously encountered situations a new situation is. Doing so puts the client in a better position to recognize whether part or all of the patterns that he or she has employed successfully in the past apply, or whether an entirely new response must be generated as a means of adapting to the novelty of the current circumstances.

3. *The relative rigidity or flexibility of responses.* Rigidity has been described as a fundamental component of depression. A depressed client must think about and establish reasonable choices in response to the questions, "Can I establish a 'one size fits all' response to situations like this? Or must I recognize that just as circumstances differ, my responses to various circumstances must also differ?"

To return to the previous example, in some ways all cocktail parties are the same, but in other ways, each one is different. Can one take a "one size fits all" approach to cocktail parties in general? Or must one adapt to each party and generate new and different ways of acting, however slight, in each circumstance? The depressed client is encouraged to recognize that there are few situations in which one can respond in the same way each time, and that one thus needs to evolve a flexible and adaptable means of regulating one's responses.

4. *Defining success.* Too often the depressed client is so immersed in negative self-evaluations that the client doesn't recognize when he or she is succeeding at something. Consider the so-called "impostor

phenomenon," in which highly skilled individuals who are very good at what they do feel as though they are impostors (Clance, 1985). They nervously await discovery as frauds when, in fact, they are not frauds. They succeed because of themselves, not in spite of themselves. But, because they have either an unrealistic definition or none at all of what a satisfactory response is in a given circumstance, negative self-evaluation on an inaccurate basis is perpetuated. It is important to help the person define how he or she will know whether or not he or she is being successful. One would have to be aware of and responsive to various types of feedback, and not just to one's feelings, to reach a realistic definition of exactly what constitutes a satisfactory level of response.

5. *The need for more information or alternatives.* Given the typically low frustration tolerance of the depressive, if the person attempts some behavior, new or old, that does not immediately attain the desired result, and also is prone to personalization (i.e., concluding that he or she is a failure), he or she may be unable to mobilize any further effort to change. A fundamental goal of treatment, then, is to convince the depressed individual that what he or she wants to accomplish (i.e., a good relationship, financial security, greater professional satisfaction) probably can be accomplished, *if the strategy employed is appropriate and effective.*

It is important for my clients to know that when they try to do something, the fact that it doesn't work doesn't mean that it can't be done; it simply highlights a need for more information or more alternatives in order to generate a different strategy. This notion can be reinforced hypnotically through the directives assigned to the client, as well as through open discussion about what the individual wants and how to gather the necessary information to build a reasonable set of alternatives for attaining the desired goals.

Hypnosis can be a fundamental part of integrating and adapting to feedback. Typically, it involves guiding the inner associations of the client; most hypnotic processes encourage a strong internal focus on various dimensions of internal experience. Building an internal focus can be most valuable in teaching self-awareness and self-acceptance. However, hypnosis as a focusing technique can also be used to build an external focus. In this stage of treatment, a counterbalance to the typical internal preoccupation is encouraged by suggesting that the individual start to develop more of an external focus, that is, to better recognize feedback from the world around him or her that will help shape better responses to life experiences.

In a sense, this process is not unlike what I would encourage in individual practitioners employing hypnosis. When one works hypnotically with a client, it is desirable to be highly attentive to the client's responses, to the extent that one could easily describe the clinician as also being in a trance state! The idea that the clinician is in a trance state means that he or she is deeply but externally absorbed in the client's experience. Only by being so externally oriented can the clinician pick up every nuance of the experience, including coloration changes, muscle shifts, and other subtle, nonverbal indicators as to the quality of the hypnotic trance. Similarly, when the client is in situations that require attentiveness and observational skill, hypnosis can be employed to help build an external orientation (i.e., attentiveness) to the kinds of contextual cues or demands that will increase the likelihood of the client's assimilating the cues and responding appropriately to them with positive consequences.

The facilitation of an external orientation hypnotically has therapeutic value in and of itself, since it represents a pattern interruption of the client's usual internal focus (on distress). Compare this with the "common sense" advice that was typical of treatment for depression in earlier decades, with depressed individuals being urged to engage in such activities as exercise, volunteering at a hospital, and joining some organization. "Folk remedies" for depression such as these involve saying to the client, in essence, "Get out of yourself." The value of teaching the depressed client to be able to shift focus from internal to external and back to internal *at will* further establishes a greater sense of personal control. One can pay attention to outside things or to internal things, as the situation warrants. Hypnosis is a potent focusing tool that can be used skillfully to help the client recognize what must be attended to and what will become problematic if ignored.

Incorporation

Once the client has had the opportunity to learn and experiment with new choices, and to discover the appropriateness and efficacy of new responses, the client is able to move to the stage of incorporating these new responses into his or her behavioral (or emotional, relational, etc.) repertoire. When the client integrates new behaviors or patterns skillfully and sensitively, it can often be helpful for the client to recognize that there is a clear difference between what he or she might have done in the past in such circumstances and what he or she can do now. It is a supportive reminder to the individual that when one tries something new, the results will also be new.

The Limits of Generalizations

It is important at the final stage of treatment that the client understand that the things he or she has now learned to do more effectively in response to various life demands are simply new responses that fit current contexts. The client should not conclude that the new responses and patterns are rigid "one size fits all" approaches to managing life circumstances. Such a conclusion would lead to relapse. On the contrary, the client is taught that the things that have provided solutions and relief now may not continue to do so later; if and when that happens, the client knows that it again will be necessary to adapt, not become depressed.

It is normal to have to adapt continually to changing life circumstances; such an ability is a prerequisite to long-term mental health. Good mental health does not mean one never has problems; rather, it refers to how long it takes one to recognize problems and respond to them effectively with adaptive responses. Thus, the depressed client needs to know unequivocally that although current problems have been resolved and therapy has been successful, the new patterns learned may not continue to work forever. In future contexts, other familiar patterns may suffice, or the person may discover that he or she needs more information, more alternatives, and some temporary help in solving new problems. What will always be different about such future-problem situations is that the individual will now understand that he or she is not cursed or predestined to fail, and that when the problem is approached in a new and effective way, it is likely to be resolved. Thus, the sidetrack into a painful loop of self-doubt, self-blame, guilt, feelings of inadequacy, and all the other hurtful things that depressives tend to experience can be bypassed in favor of moving directly to problem solving, with or without the guidance of the clinician.

In this final stage of treatment, the client is able to review key learnings about his or her own individual patterns, including value preferences and other dimensions of experience that define the client as an individual. Furthermore, the person can preview how changing life circumstances can be responded to effectively in the future.

TERMINATION

Treatment can be appropriately and reasonably terminated when the individual has demonstrated the mastery necessary to manage life situations effectively with minimal or no direction by the clinician. When the client has recognized opportunities to move into a growth-oriented phase by actively seeking new situations to broaden his or her range of skills, the clinician can have a high level of confidence that the client is no longer the rigid and narrow individual who met particular life situations in a restricted and dysfunctional way. Ideally, the client demonstrates the ability actively to seek out and manage life experiences with sensitivity to his or her own needs, counterbalanced by an awareness of and responsiveness to various situational demands. As always, termination is approached sensitively and with the encouragement that if circumstances arise in a client's life that suggest the need for input from an outside source, the clinician will be available.

The process of psychotherapy with depressed individuals cannot be of interminable length or diffuse in focus. The client is hurting and needs direction to escape the hurt and effectively address life's problems. The role of the clinician is especially important at the outset of treatment, when the client typically is floundering and needing the most guidance. The stages of therapy described in this chapter represent the goals of treatment in a suggested sequence for their eventual accomplishment. The stages of treatment described indicate when to focus on and build strength in each of the areas that eventually will constitute an integrated treatment plan. This structured and goal-oriented approach encourages the client to discover that he or she is capable of far more than previously realized, and that life need not be overwhelming, nor depression an inevitable experience.

7

The Role of Expectancy in Treating Depression

One of the most troublesome aspects of the human makeup is the limited ability to anticipate the consequences of our actions realistically. If one considers the state of the world today, one sees the evidence of human shortsightedness everywhere. We realize that the planet's natural resources are irreplaceable, and yet we continue to abuse them. For the sake of short-term convenience, we pollute our waters and air, and hunt entire species to extinction. For short-term satisfaction, we risk disease and death by smoking cigarettes, taking drugs, and finding countless other ways to abuse ourselves. The longer-term negative consequences seem to be so far removed from the focus on the now as to be invisible.

It is unfortunate that people are not taught to be future oriented. Learning to think in terms of eventual consequences and how to extrapolate current conditions into future probabilities is necessary to our survival. Yet the overwhelming pressures of socialization continue to instill in us an emphasis on immediacy, regardless of the cost in the long run.

In their book *New World, New Mind* (1989), Robert Ornstein and Paul Ehrlich present a strong case for the notion that the inability to anticipate consequences in a meaningful way is not only a product of socialization, but also of biology, specifically neurology. Ornstein and Ehrlich observe that the human nervous system is organized to best respond to the novelty and intensity of a stimulus, and that the habituation ("tuning out" of ongoing stimuli) that occurs in each of our sensory systems also occurs in response to our immediate environment. Thus, the novelty of a "Baby Jessica" falling into a well can dominate national headlines and television time, while far more profound events have been taking place: more animal and plant species have become extinct, more people have died of starvation, and more people have been born, adding to an already overpopulated planet. These significant events have become so commonplace that they go unnoticed, in comparison with the drama of the baby in the well.

I believe that Ornstein and Ehrlich have made an important point in a context seemingly unrelated to therapy that has profound implications for the mental health profession. Mental health professionals have stressed the importance of "getting in touch with one's feelings." We have encouraged people to "get the most out of life today," even if, over the long run, that advice leads to increased divorce rates, the breakup of families, the violation of traditional legal and moral standards of behavior, and other examples of courting long-term decline in the interest of achieving short-term gain. The mental health profession has unwittingly facilitated the cultural emphasis on immediate gratification at the expense of longer-term quality of life. The emphasis on "here and now" and "living one day at a time" is a philosophical position with potentially dire consequences. The mental health profession will have to accept its share of the responsibility for helping to establish a set of hazardous values and perspectives for society in the name of fostering "mental health."

When we consider the emphasis on immediacy, as well as the mental health profession's continuing extraordinary preoccupation with clients' childhood experiences as the focus of therapy, it is easy to appreciate how people can become so intensely oriented to the past and the present, while grossly misrepresenting or underestimating the future. And there is no human condition in which this is more apparent than in clinical depression. *Of all of the most important factors underlying depression, none are more powerful or wider in scope than the depressed person's orientation toward his or her own future.*

TEMPORAL ORIENTATION

The pattern of temporal orientation was described in *When Living Hurts* as a person's preferred or most heavily relied upon orientation to a specific sphere of time. A temporal component is a part of virtually every experience. After all, every human experience occurs at some point in time, and the person's orientation to time is related to that particular context. When we consider the role of temporal orientation in psychopathology in general, we see that it is a fairly obvious component of any disorder. For example, a structural component of anxiety disorders is a future temporal orientation: the anxious individual anticipates (orients to) the future in such a way so as to create images (or internal dialogue or feelings) about events that have not yet occurred. Thus, when a person is phobic about airplanes, for example, he or she is creating images of himself or herself boarding an airplane, which susequently crashes, causing the person to suffer a violent death. He or she then has all the associated anxious feelings as if the event actually were occurring! (This is an example of a negative use of imagery.) Clearly, the individual has never been in a fatal airplane crash, and so is not flashing back to actual past memories, but only to their anxiety-provoking associations.

In contrast to anxiety disorders, in impulse disorders, the overwhelming emphasis is on the immediacy of experience—a present temporal orientation. The person is not particularly attached to either past tradition or future consequences. Rather, it is the emphasis on here-and-now experience that governs the impulsive need for immediate gratification.

In the case of depression, the emphasis is overwhelmingly on a past temporal orientation. The depressive is continually hashing and rehashing old traumas, including rejections, humiliations, disappointments, and perceived injustices—and, in essence, all the hurtful things from the past. Furthermore, the individual relies heavily on past experience as the reference point for interpreting both the present and future. Even when a depressed individual focuses on what is going on now or anticipates what is going to happen later, he or she does so by projecting the past into the present and future. Thus, it is quite typical to hear depressed clients say such things as, "I'll never have a good job. How do I know? Because I've never had one," or "I'll never have a good relationship. How do I know? Because I've never had one."

The excessive preoccupation with the past is indulged in at the expense of being able to orient to the future in a positive way. To create the illusion that the future is simply more of the past is precisely the mechanism that fuels the hopelessness that is the hallmark of depression. Martin Seligman (1989) described this in terms of a "stable attributional style." Aaron Beck (1967) described what he called the "negative triad of depression," in which the typical depressed individual manifests three critical characteristics: negative interpretations of events, negative self-evaluations, and negative expectations. As a core component of depression, negative expectations demand the attention of the clinician, whose task it is to address the painfully narrow range of the client's abilities to relate meaningfully to the future.

The absence of positive expectations aggravates the hopelessness and despair of depression. It is equally clear that the depressed individual's hashing and rehashing of the negative past also helps to maintain depression. Thus, therapy must accomplish two things very quickly: (1) it must build positive expectations, that is, orient the depressed individual to the recognition that the future is *not* simply more of the same painful past or present; and (2) it must help the person compartmentalize the past and deemphasize its power in controlling the future.

In simple terms, *when the structure of the solution matches the structure of the problem, therapy is highly unlikely to succeed.* In the case of treating depressives, when a fundamental component of the depression is the depressed person's inability to develop a more positive future by focusing overwhelmingly on the negative past, it is inadvisable, perhaps even antitherapeutic, to immerse the person in more of the past ("Let's talk about your childhood") to the exclusion of teaching the person how to expand his or her range of future-oriented skills. An overemphasis on the past limits, and may even impair, one's orientation to the future. The depressed client already knows how to focus on the past. What he or she does not know how to do is to build a future that is more satisfying and beneficial than the past has been. Thus, it is strongly urged that we start to reconsider the conventional wisdom that suggests that therapy must invariably focus upon the past. It is not coincidental that the psychotherapies that have proved most powerful and consistent in treating depression not only deemphasize the past, but actively encourage setting realistic goals—a future orientation—and expending consistent effort in the direction of reaching them.

The negative expectations for the future that characterize depression are the essence of hopelessness. Hopelessness leads one to believe that the future is uncontrollable and holds no possibility for anything but more pain and anguish. There is no better predictor of suicide than a person's degree of hopelessness (Beck et al., 1985, 1990). To a person who believes that the future holds no positive possibilities, but only more unbearable pain, suicide seems like a reasonable option. The inability to create realistic images of a positive future, in conjunction with a global cognitive style, creates overwhelmingly painful feelings that lead the person to want the ultimate relief that suicide seems to promise.

STABLE ATTRIBUTIONAL STYLE

One way to characterize a person's interpretations of experience (attributions) is according to the relative degree of permanence of that circumstance as perceived by the individual. The term "stable attributional style" refers to the perception that whatever circumstances currently exist will continue to exist. The individual literally believes, "It will always be this way." When the individual holds the notion that his or her experience is not changeable, and hence "stable," the effect is most profound relative to the onset and maintenance of the depressed condition. Stable attributional style is the essence of hopelessness. It reflects the viewpoint that there is no basis for believing or anticipating that there will be any significant changes that will lead to improved conditions, and, thus, relief from depression.

It seems virtually impossible to overstate the impact that a stable attributional style for negative events has on both the experience of depression and its therapy. Stable attributional style serves as a predictor for virtually every aspect of treatment (Seligman, 1989). Specifically, stable attributional style predicts (1) whether an individual will seek psychotherapy, (2) whether the individual will participate in the treatment in a responsible and collaborative manner, (3) whether therapy will progress quickly or slowly, (4) whether recovery will be partial or complete, and (5) whether the individual will be prone to relapses.

What is it about a stable attributional style that influences all of these variables? There is clearly a relationship between one's expectations and one's level of motivation. If, for example, we consider each of the aspects of treatment listed above that relate to attributional style, it is easy to infer why an individual's stable attributional style is such a powerful influence on the overall quality of his or her experience.

Stable Attributional Style: Effects on the Therapy Process

A person's belief that his or her experience is unchangeable has direct bearing on the likelihood that the person will not seek help. Why would anyone seek help for a problem when he or she knows that no amount of help can make a difference? It is apparent that the reason why only about one in four depressed individuals seeks help (Kolb & Brodie, 1982) is their fundamental belief that it is fruitless since psychotherapy will not help anyway. (The other major reason why the majority of depressed individuals do not seek help is that they do not recognize their symptoms are associated with depression; in other words, they simply don't know they are depressed.) The "Why bother?" attitude of the depressed individual is a direct consequence of the belief that no amount of effort will make a difference (i.e., a stable attributional style). Unfortunately, many mental health professionals have come to the conclusion that the explanation for the depressed person's lack of willingness to seek help is that he or she really "likes" to be depressed. This "blaming the victim" explanation is misguided in light of what is known about stable attributional styles.

When a depressed individual does seek treatment, the issue naturally arises as to his or her level of participation in the treatment process. An individual's stable attributional style can limit, or even prevent, meaningful participation in the treatment, because, again, the fundamental viewpoint is, "Why bother? Nothing's going to make a difference." Why would a person carry out structured directives, such as tasks and homework assignments, if he or she is immersed in the belief that such exercises are futile?

The depressed individual with a stable attributional style is likely to be viewed by the clinician as an unmotivated, unwilling participant in the treatment process. This can lead the clinician down the erroneous path of questioning the desire or motivation to change. In fact, the depressed individual wants the relief that therapy may provide, but has no experiential basis for believing that depression can be altered in any significant way. Thus, stable attributional style plays a direct role in shaping the client's level of participation in the treatment. Cooperation in carrying out directives increases as the client's stable attributional style regarding the prospects for recovery decreases.

The rate of recovery—that is, whether the therapy progresses quickly or slowly—is governed by a number of factors, of which stable attributional style is only one, although it is a pivotal one. Clearly, the presence of an associated personality disorder will slow the treatment of depression, as will other complicating factors, such as the individual's rate of learning, flexibility, and ability to apply what he or she learns, as well as such interpersonal factors as the quality of the relationship with the clinician.

As pointed out, stable attributional style is a pivotal factor in the rate of recovery. A person who believes that things cannot change is much more likely to progress slowly than one who knows that current circumstances, painful as they are, are transient and that relief is inevitable in time. The role of temporal orientation is significant here, for the person's relationship to time is a powerful determinant of whether or not he or she can allow for a rapid progression toward a future-oriented goal, or whether the person maintains a belief system (rooted in a past temporal orientation) that the past experience must be thoroughly identified and explained before one can make positive changes for the future. If someone believes that insight into the past is a necessary condition for change, then therapy may have to be slowed to accommodate this arbitrary belief.

The degree of recovery, whether partial or complete, is also a function of stable attributional style and client expectancy. One of the most serious considerations in treating depressed individuals is the fact that a significant percentage, perhaps as much as from 20 percent to 35 percent, of acutely depressed individuals become chronically depressed (American Psychiatric Association, 1987). It is as if the client decides during an acute episode that recovery is not possible. A statement like, "I'll never be happy again" reflects a stable attributional style in its implication that the current pain will always be present. Thus, since a complete recovery is not allowed for as a possibility, it will not occur.

Stable attributional style also plays an important part in the rate of relapse. If the expectation is established that a relapse of depression is inevitable, that expectation can become a self-fulfilling prophecy. The viewpoint of depression as a disease is a key culprit in this issue. Conventional wisdom from the biological viewpoint has been that depression is a "recurrent illness." *It is not that depression itself is recurrent; it is that life experience is recurrent.* No one faces humiliation only once. No one faces rejection only once. No one faces the loss of a cherished object or person only once. If the person's pattern for relating to such experiences is to become depressed, then depression will repeat itself throughout life.

From the standpoint of the depressed client, the view of depression as a "recurrent illness" would help to establish a stable attributional style; that is, the kind of expectancy that would lead the person to self-monitor on a continuous basis. Any fluctuations in mood would be interpreted as the warning signs of an impending depressive episode. The expectations established in the minds of our clients play a large role in whether a person will view depression as transient and manageable or as unyielding and inevitable.

The marked tendency of depressed individuals routinely to interpret life experience negatively helps to fuel the stable attribution that when life is going badly, it will always go that way. It is of the utmost importance that clinicians take this fact into account and make an assertive and deliberate effort to help guide the depressed client's thinking in the area of expectancy. The clinician can help to establish the recognition that few experiences, good or bad, are enduring, and that the majority of experiences are, in fact, unstable (i.e., transient). Hopefulness can then start to take the place of hopelessness.

ADDRESSING ATTRIBUTIONAL STYLE IN THE FIRST SESSION

Imagine a clinically depressed client who is feeling hopeless and helpless, and who has been suffering the pain of depression for a considerable length of time. Imagine this person suffering alone through months or years of depression, believing that psychotherapy would be unable to help. Further imagine that after enduring much suffering, the person finally decides to seek professional help. He or she hesitantly comes to therapy, and the clinician spends the entire first session taking a complete case history: family history, social history, occupational history, sexual history, medical history, and on and on . . .

It is understandable why clinicians like to have a detailed history before they begin treating their clients. However, in the case of the depressed client, this approach may prove to be a serious mistake. A client who is immersed in the negative expectation that therapy can do nothing to help, and thus delayed seeking treatment in the first place, and who is then exposed to a clinician who spends the entire first session taking the client's history, now has *experiential evidence* that therapy is not going to help. The clinician has done nothing to lead the client to believe that his or her condition will change.

The phenomenon known as the "mortality rate" in psychotherapy refers to the number of individuals who seek out the services of a psychotherapist, attend therapy for one or two sessions, and then drop out of treatment (Patterson, 1980). The conventional wisdom has been that they were "really not ready" for therapy, that such individuals were "unrealistic in their expectations" of therapy, or that the "secondary gains" for maintaining the pathology were too great. In light of all I am saying about stable attributional styles, it is now clear that the high mortality rate of depressed clients seeking therapy is, at least in part, a direct consequence of the clinician's unwittingly reinforcing the individual's stable attributional style by devoting the entire first session (or two) to taking history and so providing no intervention. *It is a primary goal of the very first session to help move the client from a stable attributional style* ("it's never going to change") *to an unstable attributional style* ("things will change") *regarding his or her depression.* Thus, even though the clinician might feel better having a detailed history of the client, it is the clinician's responsibility to initiate an intervention—literally in the first session, or at least in the second—that will provide *direct experiential evidence* to the client that his or her experience can change.

HYPNOSIS FOR BUILDING EXPECTANCY

In the previous chapter, the first active intervention stage of treatment was described as building expectancy. Thus far in this chapter, I have provided what seems a compelling set of reasons why an intervention must be provided *immediately* to the depressed client that will lead him or her to believe *on the basis of direct experience* that his or her depression can be effectively addressed and ultimately resolved. In the early part of the first session, history may be taken, rapport may be built, and the relevant patterns and issues of the individual may be identified, as discussed in earlier chapters. Toward the latter part of the first session, though, the clinician should begin to orient the client to the notion that his or her experience is malleable. The clinician can state that he or she empathizes with the person's suffering, and so wants to do something right away to begin to provide some relief for the client's distress.

A First Session Hypnotic Intervention

The following transcript illustrates how hypnosis might be introduced to the client, and provides a glimpse of how a first hypnosis session might be structured in order to start to build some positive expectancy. Key suggestive phrases are italicized in this process-suggestion—oriented transcript.

Client: With all these problems I'm facing all at once, I just can't handle them. There's just no way I will ever be able to cope. It's so overwhelming; What can I do?

Clinician: You *are* dealing with a lot, there's no doubt about it. Any one of your problems would be a lot to have to deal with, but you're having to deal with a number of things, seemingly all at once. That's why it will be especially important for you to develop a way as quickly as possible *to keep yourself more clearly focused on what things need to be done and in what order so that when you're on the other side of all this, and you will be, you can feel good about how you handled such difficult circumstances.*

Client: At this point, I can't even imagine that I'll ever be past this. It feels like it's going to go on forever.

Clinician: It may seem that way right now, but *right now has a way of becoming the past* sooner than you might think. And it would be nice to have a way to *take care of yourself and feel better* while these things get resolved, don't you think?

Client: It would be nice, but I'm so anxious all the time, and all I think of is the mess I'm in.

Clinician: Let me teach you a way to reduce your anxiety, and to give yourself a break from all that stuff you spin around in your mind until you feel drained. It's a focusing and relaxation process; some people call it guided imagery, some people call it hypnosis, some just call it relaxation. Whatever you might call it, it's a way for you to *shift how you talk to yourself, how you feel, and how you do things.* Most important, you can use it to *help yourself feel better* and handle the things that you need to handle.

Client: I don't think I can focus or relax. I'm too upset.

Clinician: I know you are, and it's these upset feelings I want to focus on for a while, since they're so much a part of you right now. There are some things I think you'll want to know about those feelings, and so you can *take a little while to just explore the possibilities.* And, if you'd like, I'll tape record the process so you can listen to it again later when you'd like to.

Client: Okay. But, what am I supposed to do?

Clinician: Just sit back . . . take in a few deep breaths . . . and let your eyes close so you can go inside for a while . . . and simply explore . . . there isn't anything you have to do . . . nothing you have to say . . . it's just a bit of quiet time for you to *experience yourself . . . a little differently.* After all, no one knows you better than you know you . . . and you know yourself well enough to know *how good it can feel* to you . . . to sit quietly . . . with nothing to have to do . . . nothing to have to experience . . . just allowing the experience of noticing what happens . . . *when your body begins to relax* . . . when *your thoughts start to comfortably drift* . . . to no place in particular . . . or perhaps some place in particular . . . what *you can look forward* to being . . . that might be far away . . . or just seem far away . . . until you have the experience of actually being there . . . when what used to seem so far away becomes so wonderfully immediate . . . and isn't that the way life experience is? After all, you know how a young child is so caught up . . . in day-to-day living . . . he really hasn't learned yet to *think about the future* . . . he only knows what's now . . . and when you tell him you'll take him someplace special next week . . . he's so impatient . . . because to a child next week seems like it's a hundred years away . . . but children get older . . . and wiser . . . and no one can change that fact . . . and children grow into teenagers . . . and teenagers grow into young adults . . . and *change is inevitable* . . . so why not *choose what kinds of changes* . . . and you know how to do that . . . because even just last year you moved here from back

East . . . and you might not have thought much about it . . . just yet . . . but *there are an awful lot of things to handle, seemingly all at once* . . . when you move . . . and *change your life for the better* . . . with *new opportunities* . . . *new goals* . . . and you didn't know exactly how you'd like your new home . . . or exactly how your new friends would be . . . but you were confident enough *you could adjust* . . . and *grow to be comfortable* . . . and *you made the move* successfully . . . because *you planned* . . . and *took some calculated, intelligent risks* . . . and *the ability to plan* . . . and *take calculated, intelligent risks* . . . is still a part of you . . . though you haven't paid much attention to it . . . but *you can begin to plan now* . . . step by step . . . which *things to address first* . . . and which *things to address later* . . . which *things you can do a lot about* . . . and which *things you can do nothing about* . . . and as you *look ahead to ways you can use your ability to plan* . . . and your ability to be *so much clearer about where you're going* . . . and *what you're going to do* . . . the deeper part of you that already knows that there's *a different and better quality of life that's going to emerge* . . . and give you *a comfortable feeling inside* . . . while *you're handling things outside* . . . and so you can notice how your breathing has slowed . . . your pulse rate has slowed . . . your muscles have relaxed . . . your thoughts have slowed . . . and you *can turn them to the future* . . . of ways *your ability to plan* . . . and *take calculated, intelligent risks* . . . like when you moved here . . . as smoothly as you did . . . so that *your next move* . . . through this period of your life . . . *can be even smoother* . . . and when you know that . . . deeply within yourself . . . you can absorb that learning . . . and *use it in more ways than you might consciously realize* . . . to *surprise yourself in the best of ways* . . . so take whatever time you'd like to complete this experience for yourself . . . and then you can reorient yourself at a gradual, comfortable rate . . . and allow your eyes to open whenever you're ready to . . .

Client: (Slowly reorients.) That felt good. I heard everything you said, though. Was I supposed to?

Clinician: Of course you heard everything. And since it's on tape, you'll get to hear even more of everything you think you heard all of!

Client: That was nice. I feel so much more relaxed. And you know,

I never really thought about moving out here as much of an accomplishment before, but I guess it really is. I liked that. And I can look at the stuff I'm dealing with now in that way—like stuff I just have to move through.

This transcript provides an example of how hypnosis can be introduced to the depressed client, and how the first hypnosis process can be conducted with the goal in mind of helping the client recognize that his or her experience is not stable (i.e., unchangeable), but is, in fact, unstable (i.e., changeable). The necessity for establishing positive expectancy right away, in the first session, should now be apparent, given how much the client's stable attributional style affects every aspect of the treatment process.

Treatment cannot progress well if the client's stable attributional style regarding negative experiences is not effectively addressed. In other words, I cannot expect my client to participate fully in the treatment, carry out my directives, experiment with behaviors, and integrate the learnings if he or she continues to maintain the belief that nothing is going to make a positive difference.

The hypnotic structure for building expectancy emphasizes structured learning experiences of a positive nature, using one's resources, and orienting to the future with positive goals in mind. The steps in a hypnotic process for building expectancy can be set forth as follows:

TABLE 7. HYPNOTICALLY BUILDING EXPECTANCY

- Identify dominant temporal orientation
- Identify primary representational system
- Identify cognitive style
- Identify goal
- Provide metaphors illustrating inevitability of change
- Access personal transitions
- Identify personal resources evident in past transitions
- Extend resources
- Generalize into future opportunities
- Integrate self-fulfilling prophecy

The steps identified suggest a generic hypnotic structure for establishing positive expectations, both for one's future and for the therapy. Steps (and associated content) should be varied, of course, as the need dictates, but the general structure for building positive expectancy involves this sequence. The reader is encouraged to go back to the previous transcript of a building expectancy session and identify the steps listed.

A difficulty that many clinicians report in dealing with depressed clients is what they perceive as resistance. In this chapter, the emphasis has been placed on the depressed client's stable attributional style as the key to hopelessness, apathy, and lack of motivation to participate meaningfully in treatment. For as long as the depressed client is allowed rigidly to maintain the belief that experience is unchangeable, or that there is no basis for believing that the future can hold anything positive since the past has only been negative, the clinician is permitting the resistance-causing beliefs to continue.

LEARNING TO THINK AHEAD

In addition to building expectancy in order to establish an unstable attributional style, there is another important goal to strive for that is related to expectancy: to teach the depressed individual to think ahead. Too often, the clinician is so bogged down in having to address existing problems that too little time is left to notice opportunities for prevention. Teaching a client to think ahead, anticipate consequences, and project beyond immediate gratification or immediate pain is a fundamental task of treatment if one is to reduce the risk factors for later depressive episodes. Not all depressions are preventable, but many are when one has the ability to extrapolate circumstances or patterns in a realistic and detailed fashion. Most clinicians have had experience with clients who make decisions that obviously will be disastrous—obvious, that is, to almost everyone but the client. Building expectancy imparts the notion that the future is not entirely uncontrollable and unpredictable. There is such a thing as "cause and effect": I can often predict quite easily and accurately that if, feelings aside, I engage in *this* behavior, *that* consequence is quite likely.

An ability to anticipate consequences and realistically assess probabilities has enormous preventative value in the context of treating depression. There are many, many risk factors for depression. In a general sense, life is a risk factor, for as long as one is alive, one faces countless circumstances that are potentially hurtful. If one is going to have relationships, one runs the risk of losing them. If one is going to live in a human body, one is going to face the prospect of disease or death. If one is going to have a job, one runs the risk of losing political battles, and being fired or replaced. If one is alive, one faces the difficulties associated with being alive. Unless the individual who invests himself or herself emotionally in things that are uncontrollable, frivolous, or hazardous, or otherwise represent high-risk investments, recognizes objectively and accepts the level of gamble associated with making such investments, he or she can be stunned, or even devastated, when the emotional investments backfire. The clinician can help the client identify vulnerabilities, and learn to make safer investments or, at least, investments with clearer parameters (compartmentalization). Furthermore, the client must learn to recognize that an investment that fails is limited only to that particular investment, and is not (globally) related to all other such investments; for example, a client who suffers the loss of a relationship must learn not to make such overgeneralized, global statements as, "I'll never fall in love again because you can't trust men (or women)." Depressive episodes will be shorter and less severe when the individual knows how better to protect himself or herself from investing emotionally in the wrong people or circumstances.

While one therapeutic goal, then, is to establish positive expectations in the client that his or her experience can change for the better, another therapeutic goal of the stage of building expectancy is to help the person learn to think in terms of expectations, predictions, probabilities and possibilities. Only then can he or she carefully identify where to emotionally invest safely or when a situation is too hazardous and too potentially toxic to become invested in it.

HOPEFULNESS AND HOPELESSNESS

Considering the great emphasis I have placed on the value of positive expectancy, it would be easy for the reader to assume that I am advocating the positive value of hopefulness in the treatment of depression. In fact, hopefulness *is* a valuable ally when unrealistic hopelessness is a dominant theme in the depressed client's life. However, I have previously stated, and wish to reiterate here, that I am aware of no one pattern that is unilaterally positive or negative. Hopefulness is no exception to this principle.

Hopefulness is a positive and motivating force in the therapy of depressives when the client is unrealistically hopeless, such as one who believes that he or she can never have a better job or a better relationship. At the other end of the spectrum, however, is hopelessness that is realistic (and hopefulness that is unrealistic). Consider, as an example, a woman who stays in a highly abusive relationship in which she is the object of physical violence or emotional abandonment. What holds someone captive in such an abusive relationship? The answer is "hopefulness." As long as the woman is hopeful that "he will change," she will stay where she is. As long as someone is hopeful on the basis of wishes, and not facts, that the job will get better, the relationship will get better, the person will get well, or the situation will improve, he or she is likely to continue to stay "stuck" in a depressogenic situation.

It is a frequent theme in therapy to find clinicians encouraging their clients to "let go" of circumstances that the clients feel unable or unwilling to release. The clinician's efforts to pry the person loose from negative circumstances may be met with a massive counterresistance that serves to maintain the destructive status quo of the client's life. In the case of depressed individuals, often the person is depressed as a result of staying in a bad situation (e.g., bad job, bad relationship) in which he or she continuously is being hurt, but stays put because of the illusion that somehow "things will change."

To believe that a spouse will eventually stop using drugs or alcohol, that one's harshly critical partner will eventually become loving and affectionate, or that an individual or circumstances will change is certainly hopeful, but it is the clinician's responsibility to help the person evaluate the realism of the hopefulness. It is unusual given everything else discussed in this chapter, yet it may be a therapeutic goal to encourage hopelessness in the person for a specific circumstance that should be recognized as unchangeable. However, even in such cases, there is a hopefulness that conditions will improve when the person recognizes a particular situation as hopeless and then takes steps to extricate himself or herself from it. In such instances, the client discovers it is not his or her personal limitations generating the hopelessness of the situation, rather it is the circumstances beyond personal control. Thus, in the absence of self-blame, the likelihood of depression is diminished.

Hopefulness and hopelessness cannot be separated; they are two sides of the same coin. In the case of depressed clients, the unrealistic hopelessness for positive conditions evolving and the unrealistic hopefulness for negative conditions improving are common themes that surface in their treatment. A goal of treatment, then, is to introduce the notions—hypnotically and otherwise—that the future is not simply more of the same, and that the steps one takes today can result in changes that will lead to the belief (and the feeling) that life can be fulfilling and worth living.

8

Utilizing Trance in Treatment

Closely tied to the recent upsurge of interest in brief therapy methods, the equally burgeoning interest in and knowledge of hypnotic principles and techniques has permitted a broader understanding of the routine nature of hypnotic phenomena, as well as the huge overlap between patterns of clinical hypnosis and patterns of effective psychotherapy. Hypnosis is particularly valuable in the treatment of depression in its emphasis on active, directive, experiential, and collaborative psychotherapy.

Why use hypnosis? As discussed earlier, one's sense of reality is derived from a set of subjective perceptions about the ambiguous phenomenon called life. No one has an entirely objective and accurate perception regarding all life experiences. Those who are hypnotically trained tend to learn in a more structured manner that reality is, by and large, a subjective phenomenon; the role of what some have called the "everyday trance" (Erickson, Rossi, & Rossi, 1976; Rossi, 1986; Zeig, 1980a) in convincing us of the "truth" of our perceptions of reality is simply another way of saying that we tend to believe our perceptions of reality as if they were accurate. Perhaps, then, the best of all reasons to employ hypnosis is that when the "believed-in reality" leads to the experience of depression, the therapeutic goal is to establish hypnotically an alternative subjective reality that, to put it plainly, feels better. The evidence suggests that optimistic individuals are less prone to depression, achieve more, and experience better physical health. The evidence also suggests that optimists create a subjective reality that is no more true objectively, but simply feels better (Seligman, 1989, 1990; Weinstein &Lachendro, 1982).

In the previous chapter, emphasis was placed on utilizing hypnosis at the outset of therapy, even in the first session. When is it desirable to employ hypnosis right away? Specifically, hypnosis is indicated early on in the treatment plan based on the presence of two major factors: (1) the level of distress of the client, that is, the severity of the client's discomfort; and (2) the degree of the client's stable attributional style. Certainly, hypnosis at the start of therapy can be valuable because of its ability to interrupt patterns of anxiety, agitation, and negative ruminations. Moreover, the more deeply immersed the individual is in the belief that his or her circumstances cannot change, the more immediate and profound is the need for hypnotic experiences that demonstrate at an experiential level that the symptomatic patterns can and will change.

As emphasized in the previous chapter, using hypnosis to build expectancy is a necessary and powerful step in the treatment process for all the reasons described in that chapter. Clearly, the use of hypnotic age progression is a vital force in establishing a positive momentum that encourages the client to participate in treatment and to make shifts that will lead to desired outcomes. However, some traditionally oriented clinicians who employ hypnosis actively discourage hypnotic age progression on what is clearly an erroneous basis. For example, psychoanalysts Daniel Brown and Erica Fromm (1986) write:

> Age *pro*gression should be employed only rarely, with even greater care than age regression, never indiscriminately or with self-destructive patients. When asked in hypnosis to progress to an age 3 or 5 years hence, the patient who has turned hostility inward is likely to picture himself severely ill, in an accident, or dying. When that time of life eventually does come around, the patient may unconsciously feel compelled to fulfill the self-made prophecy and destroy his own life by, indeed, becoming involved in a fatal accident or illness. Patients may also make other, milder pathological prophecies for themselves, which later they unconsciously feel they have to live up to. Therefore, if one uses age progression in hypnotherapy at all, it is wise to use it only in connection with ego integrative suggestions of healthy growth and coping. Otherwise, we cannot see any therapeutic value in age *pro*gression. (p. 147)

It seems an unnecessarily narrow viewpoint to assume that an orientation to the future can only involve an extrapolation of the painful present or past. After all, as described in the last chapter, such patterning represents the structure of the rigidity of the client's problem. The clinician's responsibility is to orient the client to the future in ways that are positive and motivating. Brown and Fromm's suggestion that orienting the client to the future is likely to precipitate suicide may be a legitimate concern, but only if the client were encouraged to orient to the future with all conditions remaining the same—that is, with a stable attributional style. Of course, the goal of hypnotic treatment is to provide a different perspective—a different set of attributions and understandings— about one's experiences. Thus, in the same way that a clinician would not conduct an age regression to a trauma without attempting to alter the person's perspective of that trauma in some therapeutic way, one would not want to orient the client to the future without altering it in some way.

FACTORS TO CONSIDER IN EMPLOYING HYPNOSIS

In deciding to employ hypnotic patterns in one's clinical interventions, there is a series of decisions to be made about the manner in which it will be utilized. I would say the same thing, of course, about deciding to do psychotherapy, which also involves a series of decisions about the methods chosen and the manner in which they are to be used. In the case of working hypnotically, the factors to consider involve making deliberate choices about one's suggestion structures and suggestion style, as well as deciding how hypnosis can best be used in the service of whatever specific therapeutic goals the clinician and client might have. In this section, points that need to be considered in these matters are discussed.

The relevant factors fall into three general categories: (1) personal; (2) interpersonal; and (3) contextual. The personal factors include all the significant variables that represent the client's frame of reference. These include the individual's personal history (range and type of experiences), value system, subjective beliefs, cognitive style, and response style. These are the many patterns described in earlier chapters as well as in *When Living Hurts* with which the person organizes his or her subjective experience. The interpersonal factors encompass the therapeutic relationship: how the relationship is defined, how the relationship is structured, the level of rapport present, the clarity of the goals of the relationship, and other such interpersonal factors. The contextual factors refer to the context in which the therapy and therapeutic communications take place. The physical environment in which the therapy takes place, the sequencing of ideas and their placement in specific stages of intervention, and the timing for assigning specific directives, are among the factors.

In traditional considerations of hypnosis, greatest emphasis was placed on the personal dimensions of the client as the most significant factors determining therapeutic outcomes. Realistically, *all* the factors—personal, interpersonal, and contextual—must combine in a synergistic manner in order for the therapy to succeed. From the utilization standpoint, the interpersonal and contextual aspects (in which the therapist can recognize, accept, and utilize the salient dimensions of the personal experience of the client) are as important in treatment as the personal characteristics of the client.

SUGGESTION STYLES

Authoritarian and Permissive Approaches

The demeanor of the clinician is a fundamental component of the hypnotic relationship. In the utilization approach, the emphasis is on a collaborative relationship between clinician and client, with the clinician's joining the client's frame of reference by speaking the client's language and utilizing the client's beliefs and values in the service of the therapy (Zeig, 1980a; Gilligan, 1982, 1987). Thus, assuming an authoritarian position is discouraged. By "authoritarian," I mean a practitioner who is commanding and demanding, and whose suggestions are stated in such a direct form that the client is placed in the position of having to comply in order for the relationship to be defined as successful. An authoritarian style requires obedience on the part of the client. It presupposes that the clinician is the all-knowing holder of truth and that the client is, in essence, a passive receptacle for the clinician's suggestions. An authoritarian position assumes that the therapeutic "magic" is in the words and incantations articulated. A key problem associated with assuming an authoritarian position is that it encourages the depressive to take a passive position, when passivity is far too often a major part of the disorder. Therapy does not take place when dysfunctional patterns are reinforced. It occurs when the person learns to break dysfunctional patterns and to develop functional ones.

It is generally best for the clinician to assume a position of acceptance and permissiveness vis-à-vis the client. By "permissive," I mean that the clinician offers possibilities to the client in a respectful manner and communicates the acceptance of the client's experience as valid for him or her. Thus, suggestions are *not* phrased in an authoritarian manner such as, "You will do X." Rather, they are phrased permissively, such as, "You may want to do X," or "You may find it interesting or helpful to do X." The permissive style is precisely what discourages power struggles that the clinician is unlikely to win. Avoiding a power struggle with the client, particularly the depressed client, because of the rigidity of his or her mind-set, is wise, since the client can easily defeat the clinician *simply by doing nothing*! The permissive style encourages experimentation, which is a fundamental part of treating depression since a primary goal is to teach the client to experiment with alternative perceptions, interpretations, and behaviors.

Formal and Informal Hypnosis

A second consideration regarding one's suggestion style concerns the use of formal versus informal hypnosis. One can make a distinction between doing formal hypnosis and being hypnotic in one's demeanor. Another way of stating this relates to the discussion of formal and informal hypnosis in Chapters 3 and 5. Clearly, the word "hypnosis" need not be articulated in order for hypnosis to occur. Even those steeped in the traditional model of hypnosis recognize aspects of hypnosis in ostensibly nonhypnotic contexts. One must decide whether formally to announce the initiation of hypnotic procedures or hypnotically to deliver ideas and conduct interactions in the absence of a formal induction. This basic premise was elaborated in Chapter 4, which focused on identifying patterns of hypnosis in therapies that do not formally utilize trance.

While I advocate formally inducing hypnosis in the first several sessions for the purposes of building expectancy and facilitating flexibility, in later sessions there will be times when ideas can be introduced hypnotically without the formality of an induction. There is no suggestion here that formal hypnosis is better or worse than informal hypnosis. Rather, the point is that here is another choice for the clinician to consider carefully in his or her approach.

SUGGESTION STRUCTURES

Components of the clinician's demeanor are the specific word choices, gestures, and other communications he or she employs. Suggestion structures refer to the specific ways in which a clinician structures his or her communications for their maximum impact. Suggestions may be phrased in ways that are positive or negative, direct or indirect, and content or process oriented. There is no one suggestion structure form that is "better" than another. Rather, adapting one's communications to the specific requirements of a particular client represents the artistry of suggestion formation. The utilization approach emphasizes the need to adapt one's communications to the client's frame of reference in order for him or her to make best use of the clinician's communications. There are several factors to consider regarding suggestion structures in relation to treating depressed clients.

Positive and Negative Suggestions

With regard to positive versus negative communication structures, strong emphasis is placed on the use of positive structures. The client's negativity must be taken into account, however. Simply to provide positive suggestions ("Cheer up!") to the depressed client represents such a gross mismatch so as to make it easy for the client to dismiss the clinician's communications as irrelevant. Typically, the depressed client is giving himself or herself an ongoing series of negative suggestions that are, in fact, depressing: "You will never amount to anything"; "You are no good"; "You can't do anything right"; and countless other such examples of negative self-suggestions. Certainly, a therapeutic goal is to teach the client to talk to himself or herself (i.e., self-hypnosis) in such a way as to create a more positive internal environment. This is possible with the use of realistic positive suggestions that take the client's negativity into account and *utilize* it as a precursor to change (e.g., "You can be just self-critical enough to really want more for yourself . . . the kinds of things you can *feel really good* about").

As a final point regarding positive and negative suggestions, there is a response style not uncommon among depressives that reflects a negative, polar position relative to the clinician's suggestions. This seems to be related to the phenomenon that Beck et al. (1979) described as the pattern of "dichotomous thinking," an "all or none" framework for processing experience that leads to the *total* rejection of something that may seem only *partially* true. Thus, it may be appropriate, at times, to structure suggestions in a negative format in order to address and utilize the client's negativity. For example, this tactic might involve making such statements as, "Don't even consider the possibility that there may be a solution to your problem"; or "Don't entertain, even for a moment, that you could be feeling better sooner than you might expect." Such suggestions are phrased in a negative manner, but generate a positive response to the injunction implicit in the negative structure.

Direct and Indirect Suggestions

The comparative benefits of direct versus indirect suggestions appear to be equal, depending on how each is applied (Yapko, 1983). Direct suggestions deal in a direct way with both the problems presented and the desired responses as defined by the clinician. Indirect suggestions deal indirectly with the client's issues, and seek responses only indirectly. It is not, nor has it ever been, a question of which suggestion structure is better. Instead, it is a question of which approach is more likely to generate the desired results with a particular client at a given time. There is a general rule of thumb, perhaps articulated best by Jeffrey Zeig (1980a): "The amount of indirection used is directly proportional to the amount of perceived resistance" (p. 13). In other words, if the clinician expects to—or actually does—encounter a great deal of resistance (or other difficulty) in dealing directly with a client's feelings or problems, then it is preferable to minimize such resistance by presenting ideas and suggested responses in a more indirect fashion. However, in dealing with the depressive, who is prone to being global and concrete in terms of his or her cognitive style, the use of indirection may make the relevant learnings so obtuse as to be untenable. Thus, the clinician is faced with a challenge: The clinician must do his or her best to sidestep the client's rigidities and resistances, while maintaining enough clarity to make the relevant learnings accessible to the client. This is only one of the many challenges in treating depression hypnotically and psychotherapeutically.

The use of indirection as a means for establishing associations is best utilized with individuals who are likely to search for relevance and seek direction from the clinician's communications. If the depressed client is too passive to conduct such searches for relevance and direction, then the use of indirection will be unlikely to generate any significant therapeutic effect. The conventional wisdom in that range of methods that have come to be known as "Ericksonian" has been to "trust your unconscious," meaning that your unconscious mind will learn and apply what is relevant, even in the absence of conscious involvement or understanding. While this sounds intriguing from a philosophical standpoint, there is very little evidence in support of—and a substantial amount of evidence against—the notion of the unconscious as a trustworthy and reliable learner. Thus, hypnotic approaches that emphasize only the indirect methods, with little or no consideration for mobilizing conscious resources, are suspect in the treatment of depression.

Indirect methods can, and do, trigger therapeutic changes at an unconscious level. However, the depressed individual who already feels out of control can easily conclude that his or her conscious efforts play no role in what eventually happens to him or her. Thus, the illusory "magic" of indirection may actually reinforce the depressive's passivity and sense of helplessness. Ideally, when such methods are used appropriately and effectively, there follows a period of conscious learning (what some might call cognitive restructuring) that leads the person to understand the newly established associations and their role in facilitating improvement. The conclusion is that both direct and indirect approaches have much value in the treatment of depression.

Process and Content Suggestions

Whether to use process- or content-oriented suggestions is another dimension of suggestion structure to consider. Content-oriented suggestions involve considerable detail, whereas process-oriented suggestions pose general possibilities, but include little or no associated detail. A point relevant to this discussion has been made throughout this book that when the depressive faces ambiguity, he or she is quite likely to project negativity into that ambiguity and to experience depression as a direct result. Thus, if one is to use process-oriented suggestions skillfully, one must also establish positive guidelines for the details that inevitably are projected into them by the client. This will allow the depressed client to personalize the suggestions through the mechanism of projection, while staying within the positive general guidelines established by the clinician.

Encouraging the client to focus on suggested details in one's hypnosis sessions must be done guardedly. The amount of detail and the emotional valence of the details of the depressed client's associations are generally important catalysts for his or her depression. Therefore, unless the clinician has a very deliberate rationale for suggesting that the client immerse himself or herself in details of experience, it is recommended that emphasis be placed on using process suggestions that allow the clinician to correct *how* the person thinks (feels, acts, relates, etc.), rather than *what* the person thinks. The clinician must be careful to provide opportunities for the client to learn to change the structure of the ways (i.e., *how*) he or she organizes ongoing experience, rather than simply focusing on detailed content. In essence, the content of hypnotic suggestion is like the content of the client's narrative: It is only useful to the extent that it helps to communicate the relevant associated structures.

GOALS OF TREATMENT

The emphasis throughout this book is on employing hypnosis in therapy when the clinician has specific goals in mind that are specified in collaboration with the client. It is fair to say that although it is the client who makes clear what he or she would like to experience (i.e., less anxiety, more satisfaction in a relationship), it is the clinician's responsibility to build a bridge from where the client is to where the client wants to go. Thus, the clinician actively establishes and works toward specific goals of treatment, such as the following.

TABLE 8. GOALS OF TREATMENT

- Pattern interruption, building
- Symptom reduction, elimination
- Experiential deficit reduction, elimination
- Self-stimulated change

These goals of treatment represent a number of different facets of treatment, ranging from symptom resolution to what happens long after the therapy has been completed. Hypnosis is a concentrated means for facilitating the goals of treatment. It has been described as a therapeutic tool that has the ability to facilitate associations and/or dissociations, depending on how it is applied. Therapeutic hypnosis is a means for breaking the links (i.e., facilitating dissociation) between aspects of experience that should not be linked, such as happiness and guilt. Likewise, hypnosis can be used to establish links (i.e., facilitate association) among ideas, feelings, and other aspects of experience that should be linked, such as positive feelings and self-esteem.

Establishing goals for treatment seems a vital aspect of doing therapy of *any* sort, but it is especially true when working hypnotically. Both general and specific goals arise in the course of an individual's psychotherapy. For example, in previous chapters, I described the general goals of wanting to establish a positive expectancy and encourage flexibility in responding to life experiences.

The specific goals of treatment are typically a product of one's way of conceptualizing the nature of the problem. A cognitive therapist may wish to clarify cognitive distortions and correct faulty attributions. An interpersonal therapist may wish to teach and motivate the development and implementation of new relationship skills. In the framework delineated throughout this volume, the specific goals of treatment are identified as relating to the overused, underused, and rigid patterns in the depressed client that were previously described. For example, when an individual characteristically misrepresents how much control he or she has over a situation by repeatedly underestimating his or her degree of control in one or more contexts, it becomes apparent that the goal of treatment is to teach this person more accurately to assess levels of controllability relative to specific contexts. As another example, if an individual is too global in terms of cognitive style, a therapeutic goal can be established to teach a more detailed and sequential manner of approaching certain types of problems. As a third example, if an individual is too heavily associated (connected) to his or her feelings, a therapeutic goal is to help the individual develop a mechanism for getting "out of touch with his or her feelings" as necessity might dictate. The general principle here is a simple one: What a person does not know how to do is what hurts that person. Therefore, a goal of treatment is to develop undeveloped or underdeveloped resources in order to achieve a greater degree of balance in responding to life experience.

Hypnotic methods cover a wide range of techniques, from direct suggestion for symptom removal to more involved processes involving emotional release, insight, and specific hypnotic strategies intended to achieve specific outcomes. These are described in the next section.

HYPNOTIC STRATEGIES

The range of hypnotic techniques is as great as the range of possible communications. Hypnosis is employed to elicit and guide the inner associations of the client for the purposes of disrupting dysfunctional associations and establishing new therapeutic associations. The classical hypnotic phenomena described in Chapter 5 can be utilized in a variety of ways within a variety of therapeutic strategies. This section describes a number of such strategies and provides brief examples of each.

Accessing and Contextualizing Resources

It is often stated in the Ericksonian literature that clients have within them all the resources necessary for change (Lankton & Lankton, 1983). Although this philosophical viewpoint is optimistic and encouraging, it can hardly be viewed as an accurate representation of client abilities. It is apparent that a significant number of depressed clients also manifest personality disorders, and these especially reflect an obvious lack of relevant resources. However, it is worth acknowledging that clients often do have many more resources that could be employed in the service of self-help than they are using to their own detriment. The strategy of accessing and contextualizing resources is appropriate when the clinician is able to identify times in the client's personal history when he or she has been able to demonstrate an ability to utilize a resource that would be of benefit in some current problematic context. The following table lists a sequence of steps for conducting the hypnotic strategy of accessing and contextualizing resources.

TABLE 9. HYPNOTICALLY ACCESSING AND
CONTEXTUALIZING RESOURCES

- Induction
- Build response set with regard to memory (orient to general experience)
- Age regression to a specific context
- Ideomotor signal indicating context retrieved
- Suggestions to facilitate verbalizing
- Verbal interaction regarding memory
- Identify specific resources in past context
- Consolidate resources
- Extend resources into desired context
- Posthypnotic suggestions for integration
- Closure
- Permissive disengagement

In this strategy, the client is encouraged to identify an appropriate resource and place it in an important context where it will be advantageous. The continual need for the clinician to *help the client contextualize relevant learnings* cannot be overstated. One of the hallmarks of the concrete cognitive style of the typical depressive is to learn a skill out of context (such as assertiveness in an assertiveness training course), and then be unable to take that skill and apply it in an appropriate context. The need to contextualize (i.e., associate resources to specific life situations) is constant in the treatment of depression.

The following abbreviated transcript provides an example of the strategy of accessing and contextualizing resources:

Step	Transcript
	(Following induction)
Building response set	Clinician: Each person has many abilities . . . some which they know about . . . some of which they don't even know they have . . . and some of which they once knew about . . . but have long forgotten.
Age regression	And when you were younger . . . much younger . . . a young child . . . you had the experience of going to school . . . to learn many important things . . . and as you grew . . . it's so wonderful to grow . . . you were given more responsibilities . . . as evidence of your
Regression to a specific context	growth . . . and there was a specific time . . . you were happily surprised at being given a more grown up responsibility . . . that you knew meant you were getting big . . . and you could be so proud . . . of being big and being viewed as trustworthy and responsible . . . and when you can remember that experience
Ideomotor signal that context is retrieved	. . . vividly . . . you can signal me by raising the index finger of your left hand . . . (client signals) . . . and in
Verbalization suggestions	just a moment . . . I'm going to ask you to describe your experience . . . and you can do so easily . . . and where are you?
Interaction regarding memory	Client: At my house. Clinician: What are you experiencing? Client: My mother is there, and my little brother. Clinician: How old are you? Client: Nine . . . maybe ten. No, nine. Clinician: And what is happening?

Client: My dad was taken to the hospital from his work.
Clinician: And?
Client: And my mom is crying and I'm scared.
Clinician: And?
Client: And she's going to the hospital but doesn't want me or my brother to come. She wants me to watch him and stay home and wait for her. She never leaves me home alone, or just the two of us.
Clinician: And are you staying home and watching your brother?
Client: Yeah.
Clinician: Even though you're afraid, too?
Client: Well, my mom wanted me to. And I'm older.

Identifying resources

Clinician: That's right . . . you are older . . . and more able to see what needs to be done . . . even when you're scared . . . and you're able to put aside your scared feelings . . . and do what needs to be done . . . taking care of your brother . . . and yourself . . . in a way you can be proud of.
Client: My parents were proud of me . . . Dad came home with his arm all wrecked up from work . . . but he and Mom were proud of me . . . they even said so.

Consolidating resources

Clinician: That's right . . . they knew their son had done a good job . . . even though he was scared . . . he was able to handle things . . . and manage the responsibility . . . and you still have that ability to do what needs to be done . . . even when you're feeling scared . . . or alone . . .

Extending resources

Posthypnotic suggestions for integration

or whatever . . . because when you *put your feelings aside . . . as sometimes you need to* . . . to get the job done . . . you can be so proud . . . of doing something so difficult . . . and you have another situation happening soon . . . you know the one . . . that has to do with your job . . . and the exact same ability . . . to put your feelings aside and do what needs to be done . . . is a part of you that you can once again tap into . . . and it will be as if . . . it's just automatic . . . effortless . . . to respond in a way that makes a big and wonderful difference . . . responding according to what needs to be done.

(Closure and disengagement)

In this transcript, the client is encouraged to take the resource of putting aside his feelings in order to do what is necessary. He has previously demonstrated this resource in contexts other than the context currently of concern to him (namely, his job situation). As a result of this type of intervention, the client has established the association between the ability to put feelings aside and do what needs to be done and a job situation where the ability would be desirable. Thus, a valuable resource has been accessed and tied to the desired context.

Changing Personal History

The technique of changing personal history involves the use of age regression, specifically revivification. The client is encouraged to go back in time and reexperience a particular situation deemed pivotal in this person's development as if it were occurring in the present. In reexperiencing the situation, the client is encouraged to do so with some new resource that permits achieving a desired result (Bandler & Grinder, 1979). In other words, the client is able to go back in time and change the way he or she internally represents what actually happened. Table 10 lists the steps in changing personal history.

TABLE 10. CHANGING PERSONAL HISTORY

- Induction
- Build response set
- Age regression to a specific context/event
- Ideomotor signal indicating context/event retrieved
- Facilitate verbalization with regard to context/event
- Verbalize context's content;
  - identify specific resource(s) needed to change context/event
- Reexperience context/event with additional resource(s)
- Amplify and associate feelings, images of new outcome to old event
- Consolidate new representation and facilitate integration
- Closure
- Disengagement

The following abbreviated transcript is of a changing personal history session with a woman who felt depressed and guilty about having made the decision to be childless. Her decision greatly disappointed her parents, whose greatest wish was to be grandparents. She was encouraged to go back in time and reexperience the circumstances leading to her decision, but this time changing the flow of circumstances in such a way so as to lead her to comply and have children.

Step	**Transcript**
	(Following induction)
	Clinician: And it is a wonderful capability . . . to be able to imagine
Building response set	. . . and experience an imagination . . . that can seem so real . . . and when you think about your life . . .
Age regression	and the ways it has been . . . that
Regression to specific context	you wanted it to be . . . you can remember . . . vividly . . . going back in time . . . to a very specific time and place . . . when you first became aware . . . of very strong

feelings . . . and very strong insights . . . that your path was different from others . . . who wanted the experience of motherhood . . . and you can be in that time and

Ideomotor signal

place . . . now . . . and let me know you are in that experience by nodding your head . . . (client nods) . . .

Facilitating verbalization

and you can describe where you are . . . and what's going on within you and around you . . . easily . . . deepening your experience with each word you say . . .

Verbalization of context's content

Client: I'm in my second year in college . . . I'm living in a house with three roommates, women I really like and respect . . . and we're sitting around one night . . . and the subject of marriage and kids naturally comes up . . . and they all make jokes about men . . . and how the only reason they get married is for a regular sex partner . . . and I ask each of them if they want children and they all say, "Of course . . ." and I can't understand how they know that already . . . I want to get my degree . . . travel . . . work . . . have a career . . . and all of a sudden I realize I'm the only one thinking that . . . and I go home and tell my parents that I don't think I want a family . . . and they say I have a lot of growing up to do . . . and why should they send me to college if all I'm learning is only making me more immature . . . I feel so . . . defective . . . like something is terribly wrong with me . . . and I hurt my parents . . . who only want me to have a husband and kids . . . and it hurts to know I'm just not able to do

that . . . it's just not what I want . . .
I feel so selfish and bad . . .

Identifying resource (conformity)
to be added

Clinician: And you can certainly
wonder . . . in very vivid ways . . .
what it would be like to be like
everyone else . . . like your
roommates.

Client: I *do* wonder.

Suggestions to reexperience old
context with new resource

Clinician: You can be in that experience again . . . of being with your
roommates . . . talking about marriage and children . . . and you can
ignore the jokes about men and sex
. . . and have the perception instead
that having a man is what you must
do to succeed . . . and that you want
children . . . to show you have
matured . . . and accepted your
responsibility to have children to
please your parents . . . and you go
home . . . and tell your parents you
really don't need a college degree
. . . that you've met a man and want
to marry him and have children
with him.

Client: Their reaction isn't what I
expect . . . They tell me they want
me to finish school . . . that I'm too
young to marry . . . that I should
wait a couple of years and grow up.

Clinician: And don't you think you
should listen to them? . . . After all,
they're your parents . . . they know
what's best for you.

Client: No, they don't! They want
me to do what they want me to do,
not what's best for me as an
individual.

Clinician: Go ahead and tell them
you'll do as they wish . . . that they

know how your life should be and you accept that a good daughter always does as she is told . . . and make sure you finish school . . . and get a degree in the right field . . . and eventually meet the right guy to bring home . . . to get your parents' blessings for marriage . . . and have children . . . that you build your life around.

Client: I can't do this! I have to live my life my way . . . How can I be exactly what they want me to be?

Amplifying and associating feelings

Clinician: The feelings of giving you up for what they want you to be are powerful feelings. . . .

Client: Yes.

Clinician: . . . that highlight the self-awareness and wisdom of your decision *for you* . . . and you know you better than anyone else ever will.

Client: That's right . . . no one else can feel my feelings.

Consolidation and integration

Clinician: And so when you see your parents . . . and you become absorbed in the feelings of love for them, but also the powerful recognition that your life is yours . . . and they gave it to you to live your way . . . you can be sensitive to their disappointment . . . but maintain the powerful recognition that your life . . . lived any other way than how you've lived it . . . wouldn't have been your life.

(Closure and disengagement)

In this transcript, the client has the experience of complying with her parents' wishes instead of choosing her own path, establishing entirely new emotional associations (i.e., personal strengths, self-awareness, and self-acceptance) to that old memory. Establishing a new emotional association to an old memory is what gives this strategy its therapeutic power.

Critical Incident Process

As future oriented as I have encouraged clinicians reading this book to be in their treatment of depressed clients, it is a virtual impossibility to treat depressed individuals without having to spend at least some time on past issues and past traumas. The critical incident process is a therapeutic strategy for addressing past traumas. Relative to depression, it is usually not so much what actually happened that is important, as what the person concluded about the traumatic episode, that is, the attributions formed about its cause and meaning. The following table outlines the structure of critical incident techniques.

TABLE 11. HYPNOTIC CRITICAL INCIDENT PROCESS

- Induction, establish anchor to comfort
- Age regression to context
- Exploration of context
- Elicit affective associations
- Catharsis
- Identify central distortion(s)
- Dissociation of affect
- Dimensional shifting of representation/reframing
- Restructuring of focus and memory content
- Amplification of alternative representation(s)
- Age progression with new resource
- Posthypnotic suggestion for future accessing
- Reorientation

The critical incident process is invariably an emotionally charged one in which there may be a considerable amount of ventilation of pent-up feelings. Far more important, though, is that the clinician deliberately focus on shifting perceptions and causal attributions concerning the experience (reframing). It is a decidedly interactional strategy that necessitates ongoing dialogue while the client is in hypnosis.

The following transcript provides an example of the key portions of a critical incident process. The client is reexperiencing, via age regression, the traumatic episode in which his wife of four years left him for another man. This event took place about one year earlier.

Step	Transcript
	(Following induction)
Anchor to comfort	*Clinician:* And you know that I am here with you . . . in a place that is safe . . . and comfortable . . . where you can feel safe . . . and comfort-
Age regression to context	able . . . when you want to . . . or need to . . . and you can go back in time . . . to that time . . . when Mary told you she was leaving . . . and you
Exploration of context	can remember when . . . and where you were . . . and what you were aware of . . .
	Client: She has come to see me at work to tell me there . . . probably so I won't make a scene . . .
Eliciting affective associations	*Clinician:* And as you listen to what she tells you, you can describe your feelings.
	Client: (beginning to sob) She tells me she loves me but isn't in love with me . . . she's in love with someone else . . . I'm devastated . . . so hurt . . . I can't believe it.
	Clinician: And she tells you more, doesn't she?
	Client: She says I've never really satisfied her . . . I'm stunned . . . she has never said anything like that . . . I thought things were fine . . . I'm confused . . . don't know what to think . . . what's real.

Clinician: And she blames you for her leaving?

Client: Yes . . .

Clinician: And are you?

Catharsis

Client: I must be. She left me, didn't she? (crying) . . .

Identifying central distortion

Clinician: So you are entirely responsible for her leaving you? And what of her relationship with the man she left you for?

Client: I guess things didn't work out. I heard she is living with someone new now.

Dissociation of affect

Clinician: Your feelings aside . . . way aside . . . does that suggest anything to you about her relationship skills?

Client: What do you mean?

Reframing

Clinician: Why didn't she tell you she wasn't happy? Why didn't she talk to you about ways to improve the relationship?

Client: I guess she thought I was too hopeless.

Restructuring

Clinician: Didn't she have some responsibility to communicate with you if there was a problem? Didn't she need to have the ability to face issues and work to solve them?

Client: Well, *I* thought so. I wanted to, but she didn't. She said if we had to work at marriage then it wasn't meant to be.

Clinician: And when you think of how irresponsible her approach is, how do you feel?

Restructuring

Client: Irresponsible? I never thought of her that way.

Amplification of new representation

Clinician: What else do you call someone who jumps from relationship to relationship with no intent of committing to the work of a good relationship?

Client: You're right. She *is* irresponsible. It wasn't all me, though I'm the one who married her.

Age progression

Clinician: Now as you look to the future, you can carry with you an important new understanding . . . you're only half a relationship . . .

Posthypnotic suggestion

and you can choose your next partner more carefully . . . to be someone who can be there in good times and bad . . . automatically looking for evidence that this will be someone you can be with . . . in the best of ways.

(Closure and disengagement)

In this transcript, the client is encouraged to remember only as many details of what happened as it takes for the clinician to reframe (i.e., to form a different viewpoint of the event's meaning) the significance of the event. Remembering all the painful details is not necessary, and may actually be antitherapeutic by establishing even more painful associations. Shifting the way the experience is interpreted creates an associated emotional shift within the client, which is the basis for this strategy's therapeutic impact.

Age Progression and Success Imagery

The general purposes for conducting age progressions are (1) to facilitate a temporal dissociation that gives the client an opportunity to separate himself or herself experientially from the pain of the moment, and (2) to establish an association between some future context and a desired response. Age progression strategies can be performed in a number of ways, all of which fall in two general strategies: (1) orienting the individual to a positive future based on changes initiated in the present, and (2) orienting the individual to negative outcomes of continuing current dysfunctional patterns. In treating depressives, in particular, the strategy of orienting the individual to negative outcomes is best avoided since it is the client's projection of negative outcomes that is a cornerstone of his or her depression. Thus, in utilizing age progression strategies, the most useful application is to orient the individual to positive outcomes that are possible when specific changes are initiated in the present. The following table shows a general strategy for age progression.

TABLE 12. A GENERAL AGE PROGRESSION STRATEGY

- Induction
- Building a response set
- Metaphors regarding the future
- Identifying positive resources
- Identifying specific future contexts
- Embedding the positive resources previously identified
- Rehearsal of behavioral sequence
- Generalization of positive resources to other selected contexts
- Posthypnotic suggestion
- Disengagement
- Reorientation

The following transcript illustrates the use of age progression and success imagery with a depressed client. Its purpose is to establish a positive orientation to the future based on specific recommended perspectives she can have that will facilitate her success in her role as a mother.

Step	Transcript
	(Following induction)
Building response set	*Clinician:* Now you know and I know that no one can accurately predict the entire future . . . like what will happen in sports . . . or whether it will rain on a particular Tuesday next January . . . but as you begin to think ahead . . . to

Metaphors regarding the future

Identifying positive resources

Identifying specific future contexts

Embedding positive resources

Rehearsal of behavioral sequence

Generalization of resources

things that haven't happened yet . . . it is very clear . . . that some things *are* predictable . . . changes of seasons . . . people changing . . . scientific advances . . . you can look forward to new places you will visit . . . new people you'll meet . . . new skills you'll learn . . . new gadgets you'll learn to operate . . . and you know deep down . . . very deeply . . . that you know how to learn . . . and how to adapt . . . to changing times . . . changing circumstances . . . and it's true that soon you will be a mother for the first time . . . and you can look forward to that experience . . . that will provide countless opportunities . . . to learn about yourself . . . to learn about your love and caring for your baby . . . and how to adapt your life . . . while it is . . . changing in the most profound of ways . . . in ways that you can anticipate . . . like going to a PTA meeting . . . and ways that you can't anticipate, like your child's career choice . . . and you can easily imagine . . . in vivid detail . . . the look on your face . . . as you so proudly and lovingly hold your baby . . . and the way you will feel proud when teaching the baby to do something new and indepen- dent . . . like learning to stand up . . . or eat solid food . . . and how patiently you can answer your child's seemingly endless questions . . . enjoying them all as wonderful indicators of curiosity . . . and your abilities to learn . . . and adapt . . . will serve you wonderfully as a mother . . . and in other specific sit-

Posthypnotic suggestion

uations as well . . . that you can think of now . . . as I become silent for a minute of clock time . . . (one minute of silence) . . . and so you can look forward to the countless opportunities . . . day by day . . . where you can so easily learn . . . and use what you've learned . . . for the benefit of your baby . . . and the people you love and care about.

(Closure and disengagement)

The value of age progression was detailed in the previous chapter. *Any* strategy that disrupts the stable attributional style of the depressed client will prove beneficial. The use of deliberate age progression strategies is a focused means for accomplishing this. The cognitive therapy model is one of the many models that recognize the value of orienting to the future with specific skills firmly in place. Success imagery, in particular, involves the use of age progression, and perhaps even hypnotic hallucinations. The person is encouraged to visualize himself or herself in some particularly troublesome context, armed with new skills learned in therapy that function effectively to generate desirable outcomes. In essence, success imagery involves a reverse changing personal history. Whereas changing personal history takes the person back in time, but armed with a new resource in order to generate an outcome different from the one that actually resulted, success imagery takes the person forward in time to generate outcomes for events that have not yet happened.

One way further to utilize hypnosis in age progression and success imagery is to make use of hypnotic time distortion. When a client is guided through a success imagery and further suggestions for time distortion are added, the client may have the subjective experience of having hours, days, weeks, and even months, of rehearsal, all within a single session. Then, by the time the client goes out into the "real world" to demonstrate the new response, he or she may feel as though it is already a well-practiced and familiar part of himself or herself. Age progression and success imagery establish an association of the familiarity of a desired response with a specific context.

Therapeutic Metaphors

The use of metaphors in treatment has received a great deal of attention in recent years, particularly in the literature on Ericksonian hypnosis (Lankton & Lankton, 1983; Barker, 1985). Zeig (1980a) describes many uses of metaphors, including in diagnosis, building rapport, building an identification, suggesting solutions, and embedding directives. Metaphors are an indirect communication device that can impart knowledge and establish important associations in a nonthreatening manner. Metaphors have always been, and will continue to be, a valuable teaching tool, and, therefore, a valuable therapeutic tool as well.

The comments made earlier in this chapter about the difficulties associated with indirect methods are most pronounced when considering the use of metaphors. Metaphors can help to establish powerful links, potentially on all dimensions (i.e., cognitively, behaviorally, relationally, affectively). However, the typically concrete nature of the depressed client's cognitive style may impair his or her ability to glean the relevant learnings from the metaphor or to establish the appropriate therapeutic associations suggested by the metaphor. This problem is easily remedied, however. In those cases where the clinician is uncertain as to whether the individual will obtain the desired result, the clinician can still offer therapeutic metaphors, but may wish either to add a statement or two at their conclusion that encourages the client to search for relevance and direction within the story, or to identify, very directly and explicitly, the relevant learning implied by the metaphor. This may violate the "trust your unconscious to understand the metaphor's meaning" principle some advocate, but it prevents the client from feeling victimized by a clinician who seems to have important information that he or she won't share in a forthright manner.

In any case, the clinician is suggesting that the metaphor has greater meaning and relevance than might first seem to be the case; it is then the responsibility of the clinician to make sure that the relevant learnings are associated to the proper context. This is the chief function of the posthypnotic suggestion. This is a suggestion given to a person in hypnosis about new thoughts, feelings, or behaviors that can surface in contexts to be experienced after the session is over. Posthypnotic suggestions are the key mechanism for contextualizing desired resources.

The following table outlines a strategy for structuring therapeutic metaphors.

TABLE 13. STRUCTURING THERAPEUTIC METAPHORS

---

1. Gather information, including:
    *   Significant persons involved
    *   Characteristics of the problem, situation
    *   The desired outcome
    *   Available resources to be accessed
    *   Dimension(s) to be addressed
2. Pace previous attempts, frustrations
3. Build metaphor of task analogous to problem
    *   Select a context based on client interest
    *   Parallel characters and plots
    *   Reframe a problem
    *   Direct or indirect resolution suggestions
    *   Discovery of alternative responses
4. Mapping metaphors:
    *   Number and sequence of metaphors on a theme

One more precautionary note about the use of metaphors is indicated. Clinicians might be inclined to offer to a depressed client metaphors describing other depressed clients who eventually recovered. Such a strategy is potentially hazardous with depressives. A majority of depressed individuals view themselves as incompetent in comparison with others. To offer a metaphor about others getting better to a person who is depressed invites that person to again feel incompetent by comparison. The helpless and hopeless client concludes, "Everyone else can do it, but *I* can't."

The following transcript excerpt is an example of a metaphor used with a client who manifested an inability to set limits well in his relationships. The goal of the metaphor is to encourage the types of associations that would permit the client to recognize the need to set limits, endure any associated confrontations (when the other person doesn't get his or her way), and maintain his sense of personal integrity. Only the body of the metaphor is provided in the transcript.

Certainly you know how important it is to be able to draw the line . . . between what was then and what is now . . . while drawing a line between what was once acceptable and what is now outgrown . . . and that is an important thing for an adult to do . . . but not everyone can draw the line very well . . . and I'd like to tell you about an interesting interaction I saw recently between a young mother and her child in the grocery store . . . and you can easily find something of importance in this story that will help you . . . in ways that you will discover shortly . . . the mother was shopping with her young son . . . who was no more than 3 years old . . . and as he sat in the cart . . . his mother was deeply preoccupied . . . with making choices about which items to buy . . . and when she wasn't watching her son very closely . . . he reached up and took a bag of cookies from the shelf . . . and put them in the cart . . . tucking them behind him as if Mom wasn't going to see them . . . and when she came back to the cart . . . and saw the cookies . . . she threw her arms up in the air and said, "Johnny, you know we don't buy cookies! They're bad for your teeth, and they contain bad chemicals." With that she picked the cookies up and placed them back on the shelf. As I watched the boy's reaction, it was as if you could see the wheels turning in his head . . . for children want what they want when they want it . . . and he wanted those cookies . . . even though they may not have been very good for him . . . and so after a calculated pause . . . he began to cry and loudly scream . . . over and over . . . "I WANT COOKIES, I WANT COOKIES." He was so loud that everyone in the store just stopped . . . and watched . . . and waited to see what the mother would do . . . and she was so embarrassed and intimidated by his carrying on . . . that she hushed him up and said, "Alright, alright, *take* the cookies . . . Just quiet down!" Now what has she taught her son? . . . Only that he can put up a fuss to get his way . . . and she'll take him to a therapist one day . . . and complain, "My son is a whiner and a crier." And she won't even realize that she taught him to be that way . . . and she doesn't seem to know . . . yet . . . that drawing a clear line that is consistently

upheld is the key to facilitating maturity and growth in others
. . . and in oneself.

In this metaphor, the client was encouraged to think about setting
limits from the standpoint of a parent's setting limits for a child.
Later, when opportunities arose, the client could respond to others
by establishing firm, comfortable limits. Metaphors are a valuable
means for bringing relevant learnings to life and placing them within
a frame of reference to which the client can easily relate. In this case,
as the father of three young children, he could easily relate to the
metaphor on an experiential basis.

CONCLUSION

The many ways that hypnosis can be used in a goal-directed fashion
make it a highly efficient and flexible tool to integrate into treatment.
Each of the various hypnotic strategies has goals—especially the fostering of client flexibility and skillful adaptation to changing life circumstances. The related goals are identifying, accessing,
strengthening, and contextualizing all the different resources that
might be described as all the different "parts" of a person.

Powerfully affirming and empowering messages are given to the
client through hypnotic work. Perhaps the primary message is that
each and every part of the person, even those parts that he or she
has devalued by labeling them as "bad" and "unacceptable," are, in
fact, potentially quite valuable, depending on when, where, and how
those parts are expressed. Such messages are invaluable in their reaf-
firmation of the worth of the person at a time when he or she feels
utterly worthless. Furthermore, when the individual learns through
a variety of experiences, hypnotic and otherwise, that experience is
malleable and reality is debatable, new possibilities can emerge as
the client looks to the future with a different frame of reference.

9

Structuring Therapeutic Learnings

Any psychotherapy, regardless of its content, has as its fundamental goal the interruption of dysfunctional patterns in the client's experience and the establishment of functional ones in their place. The value of structured mechanisms in facilitating this process obviously is great. The general approach I have described thus far is a twofold one. First, I encourage the use of formal and informal hypnosis to impart specific ideas and establish specific associations during the course of each formal therapy session. Second, I advocate the use of structured learning experiences—directives to carry out—between sessions. The value of employing directives cannot be overstated. Just to provide information to the client can be sufficient at times to alleviate distress, however, the client is typically experiencing depression as a direct result of some experiential deficit (i.e., some missing or inappropriately applied skill for managing a life situation effectively) that only structured learning opportunities can address.

Directives, regardless of the form they take, are structured opportunities for experiential learning. The general goal in using directives is to provide an opportunity for the client to learn—in a controlled environment—to develop undeveloped or underdeveloped resources that he or she will need to manage life situations competently. The necessary resources will naturally vary from context to context, which is why there is no specific formula for treating depression (as though all people's experience of depression were the same). We have learned that it is far more accurate to talk about depression*s* than to speak about depression as if it were a singular entity. Thus, hypnotic and directive learnings cannot be reduced to a simple formula or a predictable and invariant set of techniques. Rather, it is up to the clinician to identify the salient patterns being misapplied or not applied at all in the client's life.

An important characteristic of directives is their utilization of real life contexts. The clinician can recognize opportunities to either create or use ongoing interaction and situations to make a point or establish an association, which is the goal in utilizing directives. Thus, there is a need first to establish a goal (as is always the case in directive approaches), defined in concrete and measurable terms. The clinician may ask himself or herself, "What is the lesson to be learned? What are the specific resources that need to be developed? What specific association do I want to establish in this client's inner world?"

Some clinicians advocate the use of invariant (formula) task assignments (De Shazer, 1985) and even the use of ambiguous function assignments (Lankton & Lankton, 1986), in order to observe client patterns unfolding in the context of the assignment. In the case of depression, however, such approaches are not likely to be useful. Invariant assignments may unwittingly reinforce the notion that there is a rigid "one size fits all" formula for doing things, which, in turn, encourages the dichotomous thinking of the depressive. In the case of ambiguous function task assignments, to use an unfocused approach that does not generate some relatively immediate beneficial result may reinforce in the depressed client the idea that things that he or she attempts to do in the name of therapy will not be effective. This may inadvertently strengthen the (negative) stable attributional style associated with feelings of hopelessness.

SITUATIONAL INFLUENCES ON EXPERIENCE

Using context in the course of therapy means either deliberately creating situations or tapping into existing situations in which the client's usual manner of responding (which is part of his or her depressive patterning) cannot be utilized. In other words, the client is placed in a situation where the demand characteristics of the context force an interruption of the usual pattern. There is also a demand to build some new response that will prove more beneficial to the individual. The value of such situational learning is obvious, and yet in the treatment of depression, it is valuable only to the extent that the improved responses generated by the experience can become appropriately contextualized in other relevant situations of the client's life. It has been emphatically stated at various points that much of what delays, or even prevents, recovery is the lack of contextualization—that is, helping the individual to extend the relevant learnings acquired from a specific structured learning experience to other situations of his or her life. The clinician needs to be mindful of the goal of helping the client to apply relevant learnings in all contexts where such learnings would be useful and appropriate. The use of posthypnotic suggestions, in particular, is effective in helping to establish a link between desired responses and appropriate contexts.

The literature of social psychology has provided a great deal of insight into situational influences on behavior. Countless social psychological experiments have demonstrated that what seems to be a reliable trait in a given individual can be compromised when a situation's variables are manipulated (Aronson, 1984). A sensitive individual in some circumstances will behave insensitively. A powerful person, in some circumstances, will behave passively. A social person, in some circumstances, will withdraw. The value of recognizing situational influences on behavior (thoughts and feelings) relative to structuring directives in the clinical context cannot be overstated. The creativity of the clinician is the determining factor as to how diverse and how flexible the interventions may be in encouraging the client to challenge preexisting beliefs (attributions, assumptions, and so forth) and discover new ways to respond to familiar life circumstances.

Consider a nonclinical example of this phenomenon, namely, the familiar television program, *Candid Camera*. In *Candid Camera* an ordinary situation in which people normally manifest routine responses (predictable and patterned responses) is altered in some way so that the subject becomes confused and responds in a nonroutine way that is humorous to the observer, who is in on the joke. For example, in one episode, a road block was erected at the New York/New Jersey state line, and a sign erected that read, "New York is closed today." People would drive up, look at the sign, and turn around and leave. Some of the more adventurous would poke their heads out of the car windows and ask whether Delaware was open.

This example illustrates how an association can be established quickly in a specific context. Though it is not useful therapeutically, it is probable that whenever someone who was involved in that episode crosses from New Jersey to New York at that point, he or she will smile in memory of being taken in by the bogus road block supposedly closing off the state of New York. *That* is single trial learning! The situation is novel enough, commands the respondent's attention enough, and is emotionally powerful enough to make a lasting impression. Directive therapy for establishing meaningful associations and therapeutically appropriate associations employs many of the same principles.

Carefully and respectfully making use of directives requires considerable planning on the part of the clinician. Obviously, not just any assignment will do. Many factors must be considered in creating and delivering directives to the client, including the need for the directives to be safe (meaning little or no opportunity for unplanned or undesirable negative consequences), relatively easy, concretely defined, purposeful, and multidimensional—meaning that they address several aspects of a person's experience simultaneously.

Another important characteristic relates not to the quality of the directive itself, but to its sequencing. The clinician who wants to impart specific information or encourage the development of specific skills or associations can use methods that will, metaphorically speaking, fertilize the soil before the planting of the seeds of change. For example, there are many interventions one could employ that probably would be technically correct, but would prove useless, or even harmful, if their timing were miscalculated.

For example, a woman who has devoted her life to her husband and family and is depressed now that her children are grown and her husband has left her for a younger woman might be told she must begin living for herself. She might be given the task assignment to do something nice for herself, like buying a new outfit. Such an intervention is mistimed if it is offered in the first few sessions since no experiential framework has been established in the client, nor has she learned to place a value on independent living with a focus on taking care of herself. The intervention is technically correct. With her children and husband gone, she *will* have to learn to live for herself. But to suggest that she start to do so so early in treatment is a badly timed intervention that is likely to result in resistance or increased anguish.

Any time that a directive is mistimed or is not properly sequenced in the overall treatment (by being introduced too early or too late), the directive is likely to prove ineffective, at the least, and antitherapeutic, at the most. This is why the therapist must take special care to introduce directives after careful consideration regarding what the directive is intended to do, what the potential for undesirable side effects may be, and whether the client has the necessary resources in place to carry out the directive. If the client does not have these resources, then the directive must be broken down into smaller segments and sequenced in such a way as eventually to lead to the desired response in a gradual-reinforcement manner.

TYPES OF DIRECTIVES

There are scores of types of directive interventions, all differing in structure and focus. These are well described in the literature on strategic therapy and brief therapy methods. In *When Living Hurts*, I offered 91 such directives that may be employed with depressed individuals. In this section, I identify some of the most commonly used types of directives specific to the treatment of depressives.

The Therapy Context

It bears repeating that directives are specific strategies employed to achieve specific therapeutic goals, such as clarifying and correcting cognitive distortions, reformulating faulty attributions, and developing undeveloped or underdeveloped skills. These techniques always occur in a therapeutic context. Thus, the reader should assume that (1) a high level of rapport is present, (2) the relationship is defined as a collaborative one, and (3) the clinician encourages—even demands—participation in the treatment process, where active experimentation has been defined as necessary to eventual recovery. The therapeutic aspect of these techniques is marginal in the absence of the sensitive and deliberate creation of a therapeutic context in which to embed them. Thus, there is no legitimate basis for ever accusing a directive clinician of being "too technique bound" or "mechanical" in his or her interventions. In fact, quite the opposite is true. The clinician is highly responsive to the needs, wishes, and patterns of the client since these are the mechanisms underlying utilization for therapeutic progress. Contrary to popular misconception regarding the use of directives, it is not a case of the clinician imposing what is "right" or "true" on the client as if in a unilateral relationship. Rather, the emphasis is on cooperative sharing, teaching, learning, and communicating as the basis for creating the context that permits the therapy to succeed.

The following table lists the types of directives described in this section.

TABLE 14. TYPES OF DIRECTIVES

- Task assignments (behavioral directives)
- Symptom prescriptions (paradoxical tasks)
- Reframing
- Therapeutic confusion
- Surprise
- Externalization
- Representational shifts

The Use of Task Assignments (Behavioral Directives)

Undoubtedly, the most frequently relied on directive structure, task assignments are structured learning activities given to the client to be carried out between sessions. Task assignments are meant to provide the opportunity to learn a specific skill or build a specific association deemed desirable by clinician and client. The task assignment either creates or utilizes a context in which a person will be able to make some discovery, practice some skill, or cultivate some new understanding. Task assignments may be written or they may be behavioral assignments.

Clinical Example

A therapeutic task assignment was employed in the case of a deeply depressed man whose depression had its onset immediately following a major heart attack requiring quadruple bypass surgery. From the time that he awoke from the anesthesia, he began ruminating about the inevitability of his impending death to the point that, upon returnig home, he spent his time sitting in a rocking chair in his living room and crying continuously. This case was described in greater detail in Yapko (1991), and involved a task assignment in which the client was required to keep a timer with him. When the timer went off at 15-minute intervals, he was to announce to his wife, "I am still alive." To appreciate the context in which such a task assignment was given, I had encouraged him to be more sensitive to his wife's concern about him, because his sitting in silence in the living room worried his wife, who felt she had to keep checking on his condition. I suggested that he ease the pressure on her by making regular announcements that he was still alive. The repeated self-suggestions worked because, after only a couple of days of carrying out this directive, he was forced to acknowledge that he was still alive. He was then better able to redefine his future realistically in light of his heart problems, and with greater emphasis on positive adaptation to his physical limitations.

Mobilizing the expression of feelings, learning information, connecting ideas to behavior, practicing new skills, and experimenting with perceptions are all meaningful ways to make use of structured task assignments. Such assignments abound in the therapy of depressed individuals. Common examples are encouraging assertive behavior in nonthreatening contexts, such as department stores or restaurants, keeping a diary of one's progress, creating a manual to guide decision making, and writing down one's goals. All these assignments involve active, goal-oriented, structured learning.

Symptom Prescriptions (Paradoxical Tasks)

Almost as frequently used as task assignments are the directives known as symptom prescriptions—which, in fact, may be considerd a specific form of task assignment. Symptom prescriptions are structured activities in which a symptomatic pattern of the client is amplified and then assigned to be engaged in *out of the usual context* of that behavior. In other words, a client's usual (and dysfunctional) pattern of behavior is decontextualized (taken out of context) and placed in another context that will not support the continuation of that sequence of behavior. By prescribing that the client engage in the symptomatic behavior (thoughts or feelings) in a deliberate manner in a context in which the person does not normally engage in that pattern, the deliberateness interrupts the pattern of the client's feeling as though the symptomatic pattern involuntarily "just happens." A symptom prescription strategy, when properly applied, mobilizes the resistance of the client against his or her own symptomatic patterns. In order for a symptom prescription strategy to work, therefore, there must be resistance within the client to mobilize. The contraindication to a symptom prescription strategy is when there is no resistance to mobilize and the client will simply comply and not have any particularly negative associations generated through the prescriptions.

Clinical example

An example of a symptom prescription strategy is evident in the treatment of a bright and successful business executive who is, by nature, very demanding and controlling. An engineer in his early 40s, he attempted to control virtually every aspect of his life, including how people responded to him, how people who worked for him conducted their business transactions, and *all* dimensions of his daily experience. He reported frequent short-term painful episodes of depression that were clearly related to the frustration, anger and disappointment he felt when things that he tried to control did not respond in the way he thought they should.

In this case, the client's lack of ability to discriminate between things he could and could not control was targeted for intervention. Following a series of metaphors delivered during a formal hypnosis session about controlling individuals who apparently were not aware that the things they were trying to control were beyond their sphere of influence, he was given the symptom prescription to "control the uncontrollable" (Yapko, 1988). According to the prescription, he was to establish a ritual to attempt to control something that most people would perceive as being outside of control, such as the weather or the price of stocks. Given the ongoing drought in Southern California, we agreed upon a rainmaking ritual that he was to practice several times every day. The point became clear to him very quickly that if he invests his emotions and takes things personally that are beyond his control, he is more likely to interpret the lack of success as personal failure and to experience depression as a result. Symptom prescription was utilized to promote a recognition, context by context, of what is and what is not controllable.

Reframing

Reframing strategies encourage an alternative viewpoint of experience. When a clinician says to a client, "Look at it from another perspective," the clinician is encouraging a reframing. Reframing means deriving different interpretations and meanings from the same set of data. This entire book, for example, has attempted to reframe hypnosis relative to depression by encouraging a different range of considerations and a different set of viewpoints in relating the two. Considering all that has been said about the faulty attributions that are invariably associated with depression, it is obviously necessary continually to encourage the reframing (reinterpretation) of daily life experiences.

Clinical examples

Reframing is a constant throughout therapy and so can be either stated to the client actively and directly, or suggested indirectly through metaphor and similar communication devices. Reframing occurs almost immediately once treatment begins by the clinician's suggesting that the client's experience can change, reframing what has seemed overwhelming and destructive as an opportunity to learn new skills, thereby shifting the client's view of things from unchangeable to changeable. A second reframing takes place almost immediately when the client learns that past failures or current difficulties did not arise because he or she is incompetent or undeserving, and that the things that he or she wants are attainable if approached with a different sequence of steps than previously used. To reframe personal failure as caused by an ineffective (specific) strategy rather than by (global) personal incompetence is a very powerful reframing that helps set the stage for continuous learning throughout the therapy.

Therapeutic Confusion

One of the most valuable contributions made to the fields of clinical hypnosis and brief psychotherapy by Milton Erickson was his sophisticated use of therapeutic confusion (Erickson, 1964; Gilligan, 1987). Confusion techniques arise from the observation that human beings want clarity and understanding, seeking out sensible explanations for even nonsensical things. Therapeutic confusion involves deliberately disrupting the logical, or linear, sequence of the person's thinking, feeling, or behaving. In so doing, one creates a confusion that is likely to increase responsiveness to external guidance. Therefore, confusion has value as a hypnotic tool for enhancing suggestibility and as a therapeutic tool for facilitating greater focus on and attentiveness to the clinician's communications. Therapeutic confusion is a more advanced technique to employ than many of the others, simply because it also can easily be antitherapeutic. The depressed client who is agitated and ruminating about what to do and when to do it is already in a state of confusion, though clearly of an antitherapeutic nature. What makes for therapeutic confusion is the search for relevance and direction in the clinician's (confusing) communications, which contain direct or indirect guidance that can facilitate the client's attaining a meaningful and therapeutic learning.

Clinical example

Therapeutic confusion was used in the case of a man who presented with chronic depression and poor self-esteem, which he attributed to his inability to get his father's approval. The man was a highly accomplished attorney who was well regarded in the community. In giving his personal history, he detailed numerous episodes of going above and beyond the call of duty as a son, all of which were received with utter indifference by his father. As he related these many episodes of positive accomplishments being met with paternal apathy, I recognized that the problem was more the father's inability to share affection than the son's own lack of worthiness. To confirm this, I interrupted his narrative and asked him to think of three things of which his father had approved. As he struggled to come up with some things that he could identify as positively regarded by his father (confirming the hypothesis that the problem was primarily the father's inability to express positive regard), I leaned forward and sternly demanded that he give me a million dollars. Startled, he responded that he didn't have a million dollars. I escalated the force of my repeated demand, and again he denied that he had a million dollars. His concern and confusion were quite apparent. I again demanded a million dollars, and watched his confusion and distress escalate. He intently searched for the meaning of such seemingly inappropriate demands on my part, and as he conducted his search for relevance, his confusion and agitation mounted when he could not immediately find a suitable explanation for my behavior. My demands increased in intensity and volume, agitating him further.

After several more rounds of my loudly demanding a million dollars from him, and when he was seemingly at the peak of his confusion, he finally realized what was happening and he asked, "Are you telling me that I've been asking him for something he doesn't have?" I promptly gave him the task assignment of asking various people for things that they clearly did not have ("Can I borrow your yacht? Can I have the deed to the White House?"). He completely grasped the notion that before you assume that someone has something you want and place yourself in the position of having to perform or beg for it, it would be wise to seek evidence that the person actually does have whatever it is that you want and is willing to share it.

The goal in using therapeutic confusion with this client was to promote precisely that association (i.e., seeking evidence that something exists before asking for it), which it successfully accomplished. Note that I did not ask what I would consider to be an irrelevant question, such as, "Why is it important to you to have your father's approval?" I do not question why someone wants something—a parent's approval, or to be in a relationship, or support from others. The reason for such desires is evident. The problem arises when the individual seeks something of value from someone who is not in a position to provide it. Thus, it does not occur to me to ask why someone seeks approval, or why someone wants to be in control. Describing someone as controlling is, in my view, not evidence of a problem. It is only problematic when the person mistakenly attempts to control things beyond his or her control.

Surprise

The use of surprise or shock may be a vehicle for dramatically making an important point. To behave in a manner that is unexpected and yet clearly purposeful is another way in which to establish powerful emotional associations to the relevant learning. The use of surprise can force the client to redefine his or her position relative to the problem(s) under consideration, and thus promote flexibility and a responsiveness to the methods and goals of treatment.

Clinical example

Therapeutic surprise was used by a colleague in the treatment of a woman who complained that she was a hopeless victim of everyone's insensitivity. She manifested a marked external locus of control that placed her in the victim position relative to other people. She reported feeling as if "everyone is dumping on me all the time." In response to her frequent use of the phrase "being dumped on," as she continued her narrative of victimization, she was "dumped on" by the clinician. As she described her experience, she was, playfully at first, made the target of a number of objects thrown at her. Shoes were thrown in her lap, which startled her, but did not stop her from continuing her narrative. Then socks were tossed into her lap, followed by rubber bands, paper clips, pencils, and other office items. With each new object thrown her way, she looked startled for a moment, but continued her narrative as if nothing unusual were occurring.

After several minutes of the "dumping," she became agitated and stood up and said, "I came here for help and all you've done is dump all this garbage on me! When are you going to help me and do what you get paid to do?" The clinician sat quietly, and while she stood over him, clearly feeling awkward and self-conscious, he let the silence drag on for a moment before he responded, "You did very well here. Now, I wonder in how many other places in your life you need to do the same thing." She immediately went from feeling like a hopeless victim of other people to explicitly acknowledging that she knew that her abilities to set limits on others were defective. She accepted the goal of needing to be more assertive in establishing boundaries in her interactions. The unexpected, and therefore surprising, action of "dumping on her" served as a powerful stimulus for her accepting the responsibility to set effective limits in her relationships with others.

Externalization

Externalization strategies involve encouraging the client to put his or her subjective reality under more objective scrutiny. For example, cognitive therapists often make use of written assignments in which clients are asked to write down their feelings and then to work backwards in trying to identify the "automatic thoughts" preceding the feelings (Burns, 1980; Beck, 1987). To externalize one's thoughts on paper interrupts the pattern of keeping them inside. Placing them outside increases the sense of control one has in first monitoring and then correcting one's patterns of erroneous thinking. Any strategy that encourages a person to test outside the self what has only been an inner thought or feeling involves externalization.

Clinical example

One depressed woman I treated believed that no man would want her as a serious relationship partner once he discovered that she had herpes. She was a vibrant, bright, articulate, attractive woman who isolated herself on the premise that the herpes made her unacceptable to men. In all other respects, she was a well-functioning individual who managed her daily responsibilities effectively. A significant part of her depression was related to her sense of hopelessness about ever having a satisfying relationship with a man when this was something that she valued and hoped for.

One of the externalization strategies that I use with some degree of regularity is one that I have come to call the "polling ploy" (Yapko, 1988). The polling ploy is a highly effective means for helping a client test the reality of his or her assumptions by shifting them from internally oriented, self-limiting beliefs to externally testable hypotheses. In this particular case, the client was instructed to go to a shopping center wearing a white lab coat and carrying a clipboard and pencil. She was to assume the role of a researcher, stop men specifically, and ask them a series of general "research" questions. One of the questions in the interview protocol was, "Would you be willing to date and get seriously involved with a woman if you knew that she had herpes?" She was instructed to ask as many men as she could ask in a three-hour period. She found out, much to her relief, that a relatively high percentage of men did not see herpes as a barrier to having a serious relationship. She still had other things to learn about establishing effective relationships with men, but her obsessing on the herpes was reduced nearly to zero after completion of the externalization strategy.

Representational Shifts

Clearly, a goal of therapy is to shift the way a client internally represents his or her experience. It is no startling insight that we as clinicians cannot change what has happened to our clients in the past. What we *can* change is the way a person perceives and relates to the experiences of his or her life. That is true not only for past experiences, but also for ongoing patterns and future experiences. For example, if a client describes depression as a visual image, such as "a dark cloud hanging over my head," this might lead the clinician to offer imagery of a different sort—perhaps rays of sunlight poking through the clouds—as a way of shifting the way the depression is visually represented. Representational shifts are based on the recognition that every experience, whether symptomatic or not, is represented on a sensory basis involving images, feelings, and internal dialogue (Bandler & Grinder, 1979).

It was stated in Chapter 5 that it is an unrealistic therapeutic goal to want to "get rid of" parts of oneself. One does not get rid of anger, or sexuality, or any other part of one's self. But one can learn to redefine and alter the way one relates to that part, which necessarily involves a representational shift.

Clinical example

Consider the example of a depressed client who has what he calls a "resident critic" living inside his head. He continually tells himself, through his thoughts, that he is inadequate as a man, that he is a poor excuse for a businessman, a sad story of a relationship partner, and so forth. The fact that the man has this resident critic is hardly noteworthy. Short of bona fide antisocial personalities, almost everyone has such a critic living inside his or her head. It is an unrealistic goal to attempt to purge the critic, as if it were possible to do so. Rather, a reasonable therapeutic goal is to teach the individual ways to limit the range and quality of the criticisms, and how to shift his or her response to those criticisms. Instead of giving the criticism so much attention, it is worthwhile to teach the person to *change his or her reaction to the criticism* by encouraging a different response—a representational shift.

In the case of this client, I asked him to engage silently in his usual self-critical self-talk, which he agreed to do. His level of tension and his depressive feelings were evident as he focused on the self-criticisms. I interrupted him and asked him to name the most absurd voice he had ever heard. Uncertain of my intent, he chose the voice of the cartoon character Daffy Duck. I asked him again to say all the same things to himself, but this time in the voice of Daffy Duck. As he silently began to do so, he could not help but laugh at the absurdity of Daffy Duck criticizing him. The auditory qualities of his normal self-critical internal dialogue were changed dramatically—a shift in the way the self-critical voice was represented. Had I asked him to verbalize out loud in Daffy Duck's voice all his self-criticisms, the strategy would have been made even more powerful by combining a representational shift with an externalization.

DO SOMETHING DIFFERENT

The directives described have the common denominator of requiring the client *to actively do something that is different* from what he or she normally does. The client is asked to attend to different focal points, search for alternative meanings and representations, and experiment with different ways of relating to himself or herself and to the outside world. Structuring experiential learnings is a powerful means for establishing the kinds of emotional and cognitive associations and behavioral responses in meaningful contexts that can serve the client in countless ways over the course of a lifetime.

RESISTANCE TO DIRECTIVES

It may seem to therapists who have had no experience with directive approaches that it is too much to expect of depressed clients to participate meaningfully in such active (and often unusual) approaches. In my clinical experience, the participation rate is very high, probably because the expectation is established immediately that therapy is going to be an active process of learning as a result of our therapeutic collaboration. In my training workshops, clinicians often tell me that they find their depressed clients uncooperative and unwilling to carry out directives they suggest. Many clinicians find their depressed clients the most taxing to treat.

Why would a client resist carrying out directives considered so integral to the treatment process? There are a number of important reasons, as listed in the following.

1. *The client's stable attributional style.* If the client is not well oriented to the recognition that his or her experience can change, then it is very easy for the client to dismiss participating in the treatment in an active way, since no matter what he or she does, it will be of no benefit.

2. *Improper timing of the strategy.* As discussed earlier, an intervention can be technically correct and yet mistimed. The intervention may miss the mark by being assigned too early or too late in the treatment process relative to where the client is in the course of his or her therapy.

3. *The client's global cognitive style.* Often, the clinician assumes, incorrectly, that the client knows and understands what is expected of him or her. If, for example, the clinician assigns the client the task of "looking for a job" and assumes that the client knows how to do this "simple" thing, the clinician may be startled to discover, upon careful questioning after the assignment's failure, that the client had no idea how to do so. The need to be specific and concrete is, it is hoped, well established by now.

4. *Lack of trust in the clinician's intentions.* The use of directives can involve humorous or lighthearted tasks. If the client does not have a sense of humor (often the case with depressives), or if the rapport between clinician and client is not sufficient to instill trust in the clinician on the part of the client, the client can easily dismiss the clinician's requests as frivolous.

5. *Unacceptable style of presentation to the client.* In assigning directives, particularly directives that are one or more steps removed from the immediacy of the client's problem, the client may perceive the clinician as flippant or condescending. It is imperative that any directive be accompanied by the clearly stated message that the clinician believes sincerely that the directive, if carried out as assigned, will be instrumental

in the client's developing mastery in a particular area deemed important.

6. *Tasks too threatening personally.* If the directive that the clinician offers is relevant, yet too threatening, the client may balk at carrying it out. If, for example, someone who is extremely afraid of rejection is given an absurd assignment that invites rejection as a way of desensitizing him or her to it, the task assignment is likely to be viewed as too threatening to carry out. Whenever an assignment is seen as too threatening, it is a clear indication that the client is not yet associated to the necessary resources. More work needs to be done before similar assignments can be utilized.

7. *Tasks too difficult.* There are few things more hazardous than overestimating the client's ability, thereby unintentionally setting him or her up for failure. Bear in mind that one of the criteria mentioned earlier in this chapter for a good directive is that it must be relatively easy for the person to follow. The depressed individual does not have much energy, nor does the depressed individual have much tolerance for failure when he or she is already feeling at a low ebb of personal acceptance. The clinician must take great care to protect the client from further failure or humiliation.

RESPONDING TO RESISTANCE

If I give a directive that a client does not carry out, I will never assign that directive to that client again. To do so would arouse the negative associations established by the directive's lack of completion the first time it was assigned. When a client does not carry out an assigned directive, I do not interpret that as a negatively motivated phenomenon. Instead, I interpret it as evidence that there was something about the assignment that was clearly inappropriate. It leads me to a careful analysis of what I might have misjudged about the client in assigning that particular directive. Taking the client's lack of cooperation as an indication of a misperception on my part is an important element of this treatment model.

To blame the client for his or her lack of cooperation, or to assume that the person really doesn't want to get better or actually enjoys his or her depression, is abhorrent to me. It involves blaming the victim for his or her own depressive qualities when those are the very problems for which he or she is seeking help. I find it far more useful (but not necessarily true) to approach my clients with the expectation that they *want* to get better and *will* get better. The lack of completion of a directive as evidence of a miscalculation on my part seems a more responsible position to take since it is my job to create a context for the therapy to succeed.

CONCLUSION

The directives described in this chapter all represent opportunities to amplify learnings and associations established in the hypnotic sessions conducted during the therapy session. The use of formal hypnosis to sensitize the individual to the relevant learnings—what some individuals call "seeding" (Zeig, 1990; Haley, 1973)—is a powerful way to utilize the hypnotic state. Posthypnotic suggestions offered during therapy sessions can play a pivotal role in the person's recognizing salient learnings while carrying out structured task assignments between sessions. In this way, the combination of hypnosis with structured therapeutic learnings represents a multidimensional set of interventions that can address both the conscious and unconscious dynamics of the client's depression.

10

Integrating Hypnosis into Therapy

For decades, hypnosis has been considered suspect in the treatment of depression for a variety of reasons, none of which are valid in light of our current understanding of the nature of depression and of hypnotic phenomena. Applied therapeutically, hypnosis may be used to facilitate symptom relief and function on an entirely symptomatic basis, or it may be used in a more dynamic and comprehensive fashion. Throughout this book, emphasis has been placed on using hypnosis in all ways: to generate symptom relief, as well as to address and resolve ongoing patterns underlying depression that surface as chronic issues in the depressed individual's life.

The use of hypnosis for only symptomatic relief parallels markedly the use of medication for that purpose. Hypnosis can be employed as described in earlier chapters to reduce the client's anxiety and agitation and reduce negative ruminations, thus enhancing his or her ability to attain a normal pattern of sleep and appetite. The use of hypnosis to provide symptomatic relief, while simultaneously addressing the associated dysfunctional patterns causing and maintaining the client's depression, is perhaps the best of all ways to employ hypnosis as a tool in treatment.

OTHER TREATMENT CONSIDERATIONS

The Use of Antidepressant Medication

The longitudinal data clearly indicate that antidepressant medication can play a significant role in alleviating depressive symptoms and facilitating relief from later depressive episodes. The data also show, however, a higher rate of relapse with medications than when the client receives psychotherapy (Weissman, 1983; McGrath et al., 1990). The viewpoint of depression as primarily a learned phenomenon, as expressed in this volume, in most cases, does not negate the value of antidepressant medication when appropriately prescribed and utilized. It seems, however, that a finer distinction needs to be made between viewing depression as having a biological cause and acknowledging that depression, like all human experience, has associated biological correlates.

The value of medication in providing symptomatic relief may best be realized at the outset of treatment, particularly when the client is experiencing a depression too severe to allow participation in psychotherapy. The data have led many depression experts, whether medically or psychologically oriented, to recognize that the use of medication as an exclusive form of treatment (i.e., without any psychotherapy) is generally a disservice to the patient (Weissman, 1983; Akiskal, 1985). Given the emphasis on the role of one's subjective patterns for organizing experience as the precursor to depression, the reason for medication's limited role may be more apparent.

Mobilizing the energy of the individual, enhancing his or her concentration, and reducing the vegetative symptoms (i.e., sleep and appetite disturbances, loss of sex drive) seem the most appropriate uses of antidepressant medication. It is recommended that in those cases where antidepressant medication is employed, it be administered with the goal of eventually reducing and then terminating the client's reliance on the medication. This can be done when the symptoms have remitted and the associated depressogenic patterns have been interrupted.

Dual Diagnosis

Studies of comorbidity are not yet plentiful, nor are they conclusive; however, there is considerable evidence that depression quite often goes hand in hand with other disorders. Specifically, there is a considerable percentage of individuals whose major depression is superimposed on an underlying personality disorder, most frequently the dependent personality disorder (Kocsis & Frances, 1988; Beck, 1991). When the clinician is able to diagnose the presence of a personality disorder coexisting with the major depression, the clinical intervention plan obviously must be altered. Most significant in such cases is the temporal factor, as the therapy will probably take longer to complete.

In this volume, I have specifically addressed major depression (unipolar disorder), advocating a style of brief therapy that can be accomplished in the number of sessions normally ascribed to brief therapy methods, namely one to 20 sessions, with about a dozen sessions being typical. When the comorbidity profile suggests a personality disorder, the treatment techniques in most cases will be the same. However, it seems unlikely that resolution will occur in so few sessions. A general principle, first described in Chapter 3, suggests that the more loosely structured the client's experience, the more tightly structured the therapy will have to be. Thus, when treating depression that coexists with a personality disorder, the symptoms of depression and its associated underlying patterns will still be the appropriate target for the early phases of treatment in order to, in essence, "get the depression out of the way." Then one can proceed with treating the associated personality disorder.

Depression is also often related to other psychological disturbances, such as anxiety disorders, substance abuse, and psychophysiological disorders (Kuhs, 1991; Murphy & Wetzel, 1990). The perception that depression is a reflection of only a mood disorder is an unnecessarily limiting perspective; an individual may have virtually all of the patterns associated with depression, and yet be so prone to dissociate from his or her feelings as not to experience any particular problems in the area of mood. Thus, the clinician, familiar with the patterns described in this volume, and in the earlier volume, *When Living Hurts* (Yapko, 1988), will be in a stronger position to recognize depressogenic patterns that indicate that either the person is currently depressed or is at risk for later episodes. The point here is that in treating individuals with dual diagnoses, the depressogenic patterns are generally the appropriate first targets of treatment.

CONTRAINDICATIONS TO DIRECTIVE APPROACHES

Traditionally, emphasis in the treatment of depression has been placed on the clinician's assuming a supportive position that encourages the ventilation and exploration of depressed feelings. However, merely offering support allows the risk factors underlying the depression to continue even after the depressive episode has ended. Clearly, there is a need for direction in solving current problems, as well as in anticipating future ones, and preventing them when possible. That is not to say that it is wrong or inadvisable simply to offer support to an individual as one's therapeutic approach. The question naturally arises of when to offer support and when to offer direction. There are indications for and contraindications to the use of both of these methods.

In general, there is only one specific time to move into the position of merely providing support. Such an approach is indicated when the client clearly has an unstable attributional style that reflects an ability to recognize the current depressive episode as exactly that—an episode. When the person recognizes that it is an acute, though painful, transient episode that is related to specific life circumstances (e.g., death, loss of a job), and realizes that these are not enduring circumstances and that the experience of depression is normal in such circumstances, this is the time when a clinician can comfortably offer support as the client passes through a difficult phase. Thus, it is extremely important for the clinician to assess whether the person recognizes that the circumstances are transient, or instead is in danger of forming enduring dysfunctional attitudes or behaviors rooted in a belief that the episode is but a sample of a negative and unchangeable future.

A contraindication to the use of directive methods is when the individual does not need direction, is clear about what needs to be done and when, and is realistic about the painful circumstances as being transient. In such cases, supportive psychotherapy alone may be adequate.

The most serious of all the contraindications to directive approaches is, in most cases, when the clinician is unable to anticipate and utilize all the possible responses that the client might generate in response to directives. Whenever a clinician makes use of symptom prescription strategies or task assignments (or any directive for that matter), he or she has in mind a particular therapeutic goal that the strategy will facilitate accomplishing. The clinician must consider, before assigning any directive, his or her responses to these questions: Other than the intended response, what other responses might the client generate in response to this directive? What hazards might be associated with carrying out this directive? What other associations might be established in completing this assignment? *If, for any reason, it is possible for the client to generate unintended or unwanted responses to the directive, then it is most respectful and conservative not to employ that directive.* The clinician's responsibility, above all else, is to do no harm to the client. Therefore, the clinician must anticipate the spectrum of responses a client might have to a particular assignment. Unless the clinician can utilize in a positive fashion any and all responses, it is wise to not use the directive.

Another serious contraindication to directive methods in particular, but to any type of therapeutic intervention in general, is when the intervention encourages, intentionally or otherwise, the client to maintain a stable attributional style. With all that has been said throughout this volume about the broad range of factors influencing the course of therapy that are related to a stable attributional style, it is clear that we want to do nothing that can be interpreted by the client as evidence that his or her condition is unchangeable. That is why it is particularly distasteful to me to frame depression as a chronic recurrent illness, or to provide labels to the client with which he or she can identify, when those labels represent a pathological and unchangeable phenomenon. (For example, does one ever stop being the "adult child of an alcoholic"?) At no time should the clinician communicate to the client that his or her condition or reactions to the condition are unchangeable.

As for the specific contraindications to the use of hypnosis, it may seem a bold statement to make, but I am aware of no such contraindications. However, I know of many contraindications to applying hypnosis in ways that can be considered foolish or destructive. The danger is never in the hypnosis in and of itself. The dangers of utilizing hypnosis arise only when individual therapists encourage clients through hypnosis to amplify destructive or nonsalient dimensions of experience in the name of psychotherapy.

CONCLUDING REMARKS

There are those who believe that the stresses of modern life are different from, but no greater than, the stresses faced by previous generations. I strongly disagree. The world—our world—is a far different place with entirely different problems than previously existed. The potential for destruction on a planetary scale is an ever-present threat—overpopulation, pollution of our air and water, widespread destruction of our planet's irreplaceable resources, and on and on. It is an easy, though hurtful, prediction to make that the rate of depression will continue its upward climb. The mental health profession has contributed to the problem with its incongruent emphasis on (1) slow, irrelevant therapies and quick-fix pills; (2) getting in touch with one's feelings and not one's responsibilities; (3) individual happiness and not relationships or integrity; and (4) the illusion of educated omnipotence and the paradoxical encouragement of victimization by encouraging people to see abuse almost everywhere.

No one has all the answers to such complex problems; after all, though this book is at its end, life forever remains an ambiguous stimulus. But, I can attempt to communicate my desire to help in the best way I know how—namely, by encouraging a different way of viewing depression and its treatment. The hypnotic framework involves different perspectives and methods, broadening the range of ways in which we can respond to the people whom we care so much about, our clients. I hope that these perspectives and methods will help.

References

Akiskal, H. (1985). The challenge of chronic depressions. In A. Dean (Ed.), *Depression in multidisciplinary perspective* (pp. 105–117). New York: Brunner/Mazel.

Alloy, L., & Abramson, L. (1988). Depressive realism: Four theoretical perspectives. In L. Alloy (Ed.), *Cognitive processes in depression* (pp. 223–265). New York: Guilford Press.

American Psychiatric Association (1987). *Diagnostic and statistical manual of mental disorders* (3rd ed., revised). Washington, D.C.: Author.

Araoz, D. (1985). *The new hypnosis.* New York: Brunner/Mazel.

Arieti, S., & Bemporad, J. (1978). *Severe and mild depression.* New York: Basic Books.

Aronson, E. (1984). *The social animal* (4th ed.). San Francisco: Freeman.

Bandler, R., & Grinder, J. (1979). *Frogs into princes.* Moab, Utah: Real People Press.

Barker, P. (1985). *Using metaphors in psychotherapy.* New York: Brunner/Mazel.

Beach, S., Nelson, G., & O'Leary, K. (1988). Cognitive and marital factors in depression. *Journal of Psychopathology and Behavioral Assessment, 10,* 93–105.

Beach, S., & Nelson, G. (1990). Pursuing research on major psychopathology from a contextual perspective: The example of depression and marital discord. In G. Brody & I. Sigel (Eds.), *Family research ,Vol. II: Clinical populations.* Hillsdale, N.J.: Erlbaum.

Beach, S., Sandeen, E., & O'Leary, K. (1990). *Depression in marriage.* New York: Guilford Press.

Beck, A. (1967). *Depression: Causes and treatment.* Philadelphia, Pa.: University of Pennsylvania Press.

Beck, A. (1973). *The diagnosis and management of depression.* Philadelphia: University of Pennsylvania Press.

Beck, A. (1976). *Cognitive therapy and the emotional disorders.* New York: International Universities Press.

Beck, A. (1987). Cognitive therapy. In J. Zeig (Ed.), *The evolution of psychotherapy* (pp. 149–163). New York: Brunner/Mazel.

Beck, A. (1991). An interview with Aaron Beck by Michael Yapko. *The Milton H. Erickson Foundation Newsletter, II*(2).

Beck, A., Brown, G., Berchick, R., Stewart, B., & Steer, R. (1990). Relationship between hopelessness and ultimate suicide: A replication with psychiatric outpatients. *American Journal of Psychiatry, 147,* 190–195.

Beck, A., Rush, J., Shaw, B., & Emery, G. (1979). *Cognitive therapy of depression.* New York: Guilford Press.

Beck, A., Steer, R., Kovacs, M., & Garrison, B. (1985). Hopelessness and eventual suicide: A 10 year prospective study of patients hospitalized with suicidal ideation. *American Journal of Psychiatry, 142,* 559–563.

Becker, R., & Heimberg, R. (1985). Cognitive-behavioral treatments for depression: A review of controlled research. In A. Dean (Ed.), *Depression in multidisciplinary perspective* (pp. 209–234). New York: Brunner/Mazel.

Bernstein, N. (1982). Affective disorders and the family system. In E. Val, F. Gaviria, & J. Flaherty (Eds.), *Affective disorders: Psychopathology and treatment* (pp. 441–453). Chicago: Year Book Medical Publishers.

Bertelsen, A. (1988). Genetic aspects in affective disorders: Introductory remarks. In T. Heghason & R. Daly (Eds.), *Depressive illness: Prediction of course and outcome.* Berlin: Springer-Verlag.

Birtchnell, J. (1991). Negative modes of relating, marital quality and depression. *British Journal of Psychiatry, 158,* 648– 657.

Blackburn, I., & Davidson, K. (1990). *Cognitive therapy for depression and anxiety.* Oxford: Blackwell Scientific Publications.

Brown, D. & Fromm, E. (1986). *Hypnotherapy and hypnoanalysis.* Hillsdale, N.J.: Erlbaum.

Brown, G. (1985). Depression: A radical social perspective. In K. Herbst & E. Paykel (Eds.), *Depression: An integrative approach.* (pp. 21–44). Oxford: Heinemann Professional Publishing.

Brown, G. & Harris, T. (1978). *Social origins of depression. A study of psychiatric disorder in women.* New York: Free Press.

Burns, D. (1980). *Feeling good: The new mood therapy.* New York: Morrow.

Burrows, G. (1980). Affective disorders and hypnosis. In G. Burrows & L. Dennerstein (Eds.), *Handbook of hypnosis and psychosomatic medicine* (pp. 149–170). Amsterdam: Elsevier/North-Holland: Biomedical Press.

Chambers, H. (1968). Oral erotism revealed by hypnosis. *International Journal of Clinical and Experimental Hypnosis, 16,* 151–157.

Charney, D., Nelson, J., & Quinlan, D. (1981). Personality traits and disorder in depression. *American Journal of Psychiatry, 138,* 1601–1604.

Charney, E., & Weissman, M. (1988). Epidemiology of depressive illness. In J. Mann (Ed.), *Phenomenology of depressive illnesses* (pp. 45–74). New York: Human Sciences Press.

Cheek, D., & LeCron, L. (1968). *Clinical hypnotherapy.* New York: Grune & Stratton.

Clance, P. (1985). *The imposter phenomenon.* New York: Bantam Books.

Clarke, J., & Jackson, J. (1983). *Hypnosis and behavior therapy.* New York: Springer.

Cleve, J. (1985). *Out of the blues.* Minneapolis, Minn.: CompCare Publishers.

Crasilneck, H. (1980). Clinical assessment and preparation of the patient. In G. Burrows & L. Dennerstein (Eds.), *Handbook of hypnosis and psychosomatic medicine* (pp. 105–118). Amsterdam: Elsevier/North-Holland: Biomedical Press.

Crasilneck, H., & Hall, J. (1985). *Clinical hypnosis: Principles and applications* (2nd ed.). New York: Grune & Stratton.

Davis, J., & Maas, J. (Eds.) (1983). *The affective disorders.* Washington, D.C.: American Psychiatric Press.

Davison, G., & Neale, J. (1986). *Abnormal psychology* (4th ed.). New York: John Wiley & Sons.

Dean, A. (1985). On the epidemiology of depression. In A. Dean (Ed.), *Depression in multidisciplinary perspective.* New York: Brunner/Mazel.

De Shazer, S. (1985). *Keys to solution in brief therapy.* New York: Norton.

De Shazer, S. (1991). *Putting difference to work.* New York: Norton.

DiMatteo, M., & Hays, R. (1981). Social support and serious illness. In B. Gottlieb (Ed.), *Social networks and social support.* Beverly Hills, Calif.: Sage.

Edelstein, M. (1981). *Trauma, trance, and transformation.* New York: Brunner/Mazel.

Egeland, J., & Hostetter, A. (1983). Amish study. I: Affective disorders among the Amish, 1976–1980. *American Journal of Psychiatry, 140:*1, 56–61.

Ellis, A. (1979). *Reason and emotion in psychotherapy.* New York: Stuart.

Ellis, A. (1987). The evolution of rational-emotive therapy (RET) and cognitive behavior therapy (CBT). In J. Zeig (Ed.), *The evolution of psychotherapy* (pp. 107–125). New York: Brunner/Mazel.

Erickson, M. (1958). Naturalistic techniques of hypnosis. *American Journal of Clinical Hypnosis, 1,* 3–8.

Erickson, M. (1964). The confusion technique in hypnosis. *American Journal of Clinical Hypnosis, 6,* 183–207.

Erickson, M. (1980). In E. Rossi (Ed.), *The collected papers of Milton H. Erickson on hypnosis, Vol II: Hypnotic alteration of sensory perceptual, and psychophysiological processes.* New York: Irvington.

Erickson, M., & Rossi, E. (1979). *Hypnotherapy: An exploratory casebook.* New York: Irvington.

Erickson, M. & Rossi, E. (1981). *Experiencing hypnosis: Therapeutic approaches to altered states.* New York: Irvington.

Erickson, M., Rossi, E., & Rossi, S. (1976). *Hypnotic realities.* New York: Irvington.

Fisch, R. (1982). Erickson's impact on brief psychotherapy. In J. Zeig (Ed.), *Ericksonian approaches to hypnosis and psychotherapy* (pp. 155–162). New York: Brunner/Mazel.

Fisch, R., Weakland, J., & Segal, L. (1983). *The tactics of change: Doing therapy briefly.* San Francisco, Calif.: Jossey-Bass.

Foerster, H. von (1984). On constructing a reality. In P. Watzlawick (Ed.) *The invented reality* (pp. 41–61). New York: Norton.

Freud, S. (1953). Freud's psychoanalytic method. In *The collected papers of Sigmund Freud* (Vol. I). London: Hogarth.

Gilligan, S. (1982). Ericksonian approaches to clinical hypnosis. In J. Zeig (Ed.) *Ericksonian approaches to hypnosis and psychotherapy* (pp. 87–103). New York: Brunner/Mazel.

Gilligan, S. (1987). *Therapeutic trances: The cooperation principle in Ericksonian hypnotherapy.* New York: Brunner/Mazel.

Gilligan, S. (1988). Symptom phenomena as trance phenomena. In J. Zeig & S. Lankton (Eds.), *Developing Ericksonian therapy* (pp. 327–352). New York: Brunner/Mazel.

Gilligan, S. (1989). The therapist as variety generator: Developing solutions with depressed clients. In M. Yapko (Ed.), *Brief therapy approaches to treating anxiety and depression* (pp. 327–347). New York: Brunner/Mazel.

Glaserfeld, E. von (1984). An introduction to radical constructivism. In P. Watzlawick (Ed.), *The invented reality* (pp. 17–40). New York: Norton.

Goldenberg, I., & Goldenberg, H. (1985). *Family therapy: An overview.* Monterey, Calif.: Brooks/Cole.

Gruber, L. (1983). Hypnotherapeutic techniques in patients with affective instability. *American Journal of Clinical Hypnosis, 25,* 263–267.

Guidano, V. (1987). *Complexity of the self: A developmental approach to psychotherapy and therapy.* New York: Guilford Press.

Haley, J. (1973). *Uncommon therapy: The psychiatric techniques of Milton H. Erickson, M.D.* New York: Norton.

Haley, J. (1982). The contribution to therapy of Milton H. Erickson, M.D. In J. Zeig (Ed.), *Ericksonian approaches to hypnosis and psychotherapy* (pp. 5–25). New York: Brunner/Mazel.

Haley, J. (1987). Therapy—a new phenomenon. In J. Zeig (Ed.), *The evolution of psychotherapy* (pp. 17–28). New York: Brunner/Mazel.

Hammond, D. (Ed.) (1990). *Handbook of hypnotic suggestions and metaphors.* New York: Norton.

Havens, R., & Walters, C. (1989). *Hypnotherapy scripts: A neo-Ericksonian approach to persuasive healing.* New York: Brunner/Mazel.

Heller, S. (1987) *Monsters and magical sticks.* Phoenix, Ariz.: Falcon Press.

Hilgard, E. (1968). *The experience of hypnosis.* New York: Harcourt, Brace & World.

Hodge, J. (1990). Hypnotic suggestions to deter suicide. In D. Hammond (Ed.), *Handbook of hypnotic suggestions and metaphors.* New York: Norton.

Hoffman, L. (1990). Constructing realities: An art of lenses. *Family process, 29,* 1–12.

Jacobson, N. (1985, August). Combining marital therapy with individual therapy in the treatment of depression. Paper presented at the 93rd annual meeting of the American Psychological Association, Los Angeles, Calif.

Katz, R., & McGuffin, P. (1987). Neuroticism in familial depression. *Psychological medicine, 17,* 155–161.

Kleinman, A. (1982). Neurasthenia and depression: A study of somatization and culture in China. *Culture, Medicine and Psychiatry, 6,* 117–190.

Klerman, G. (1988). The current age of youthful melancholia. *British Journal of Psychiatry, 152,* 4–14.

Klerman, G., Weissman, M., Rounsaville, B., & Chevron, E. (1984). *Interpersonal psychotherapy of depression.* New York: Basic Books.

Kocsis, J., & Frances, A. (1988). Chronic depression. In J. Mann (Ed.), *Phenomenology of depressive illness* (pp. 126–140). New York: Human Sciences Press.

Kolb, L., & Brodie, H. (1982). *Modern clinical psychiatry* (10th ed.). Philadelphia: W.B. Saunders.

Koriath, J. (1989). A renaissance paradigm. In M. Yapko (Ed.), *Brief therapy approaches to treating anxiety and depression* (pp. 50–63). New York: Brunner/Mazel.

Kroger, W. (1977). *Clinical and experimental hypnosis in medicine, dentistry, and psychology* (2nd ed.). Philadelphia: Lippincott.

Kuhs, H. (1991). Anxiety in depressive disorders. *Comprehensive psychiatry, 32–3,* 217–228.

Lankton, S., & Lankton, C. (1983). *The answer within: A clinical framework of Ericksonian hypnotherapy.* New York: Brunner/Mazel.

Lankton, S., & Lankton, C. (1986). *Enchantment and intervention in family therapy.* New York: Brunner/Mazel.

Lefrancois, G. (1986) *Of children* (5th ed.). Belmont, Calif.: Wadsworth.

Lin, N., & Dean, A. (1984). Social support and depression: A panel study. *Social psychiatry, 19,* 1–9.

Marsella, A. (1979). Depressive experience and disorder across cultures. In H. Triandis & J. Draguns (Eds.), *Handbook of cross-cultural psychology, psychopathology* (Vol. 6). Boston: Allyn & Bacon.

Marsella, A., Sartorius, N., Jablensky, A. & Fenton, F. (1985). Cross cultural studies of depressive disorders: An overview. In A. Kleinman & B. Good (Eds.), *Culture and depression* (pp. 299–324). Berkeley, Calif.: University of California Press.

McGrath, E., Keita, G., Strickland, B., & Russo, N. (Eds.) (1990). *Women and depression: Risk factors and treatment issues.* Washington, D.C.: American Psychological Association.

Meares, A. (1960). *A system of medical hypnosis.* New York: Julian Press.

Milechnin, A. (1967). *Hypnosis.* Bristol, England: John Wright & Sons.

Miller, M. (1979). *Therapeutic hypnosis.* New York: Human Sciences Press.

Miller, M. (1983). Depression and hypnotherapy of depression. In W. Wester & A. Smith (Eds.), *Clinical hypnosis: A multidisciplinary approach* (pp. 421–457). Philadelphia: Lippincott.

Murphy, G., & Wetzel, R. (1990). The lifetime risk of suicide in alcoholism. *Archives of General Psychiatry, 47,* 383–392.

Murray, E. (1985). Coping and anger. In T. Field, P. McCabe, & N. Schneiderman (Eds.), *Stress and coping.* Hillsdale, N.J.: Erlbaum.

Nasr, S. (1982). Suicide. In E. Val, F. Gaviria, & J. Flaherty (Eds.), *Affective disorders: Psychopathology and treatment* (pp. 229–243). Chicago: Year Book Medical Publishers.

Nezu, A., Nezu, C., & Perri, M. (1989). *Problem-solving therapy for depression.* New York: John Wiley & Sons.

Nolen–Hoeksema, S., Girgus, J., & Seligman, M. (1986). Learned helplessness in children: A longitudinal study of depression, achievement, and explanatory style. *Journal of Personality and Social Psychology, 51,* 435–442.

O'Hanlon, W. (1987). *Taproots: Underlying principles of Milton Erickson's therapy and hypnosis.* New York: Norton.

Ornstein, R., & Ehrlich, P. (1989). *New world, new mind.* New York: Touchstone.

Patterson, C. (1980). *Theories of counseling and psychotherapy* (3rd ed.). New York: Harper & Row.

Reich, T., Van Eerdewegh, P., Rice, J., Mullaney, J., Endicott, J., & Klerman, G. (1987). The familial transmission of primary major depressive disorder. *Journal of Psychiatric Research, 21,* 613–624.

Robins, L., Helzer, J., Weissman, M., Orvaschel, H., Gruenberg, E., Burke, J., & Regier, D. (1984). Lifetime prevalence of specific psychiatric disorders in three communities. *Archives of General Psychiatry, 41,* 949–958.

Rosen, H. (1955). Regression hypnotherapeutically induced as an emergency measure in a suicidally depressed patient. *International Journal of Clinical and Experimental Hypnosis, 3,* 58–70.

Rosen, H. (1981). Hypnosis. In *The encyclopedia of psychology.* Guilford, Conn.: DPG Reference Publishing.

Rossi, E. (1985). Unity and diversity in Ericksonian approaches: Now and in the future. In J. Zeig (Ed.), *Ericksonian psychotherapy, Vol. 1: Structures* (pp. 15–29). New York: Brunner/Mazel.

Rossi, E. (1986). *The psychobiology of mind–body healing.* New York: Norton.

Rossi, E. (1987). Mind/body communication and the new language of human facilitation. In J. Zeig (Ed.), *The evolution of psychotherapy* (pp. 369–387). New York: Brunner/Mazel.

Rounsaville, B., Weissman, M., Prusoff, B., & Herceg-Baron, R. (1979). Marital disputes and treatment outcome in depressed women. *Comprehensive Psychiatry 20,* 483–490.

Safran, J. & Segal, Z. (1990). *Interpersonal process in cognitive therapy.* New York: Basic Books.

Samko, M. (1986). Rigidity and pattern interruption: Central issues underlying Milton Erickson's approach to psychotherapy. In M. Yapko (Ed.) *Hypnotic and strategic interventions: Principles and practice* (pp. 47–55). New York: Irvington.

Sartorius, N., & Ban, T. (1986). *Assessment of depression.* Berlin: Springer-Verlag.

Schiefflin, E. (1985). The cultural analysis of depressive affect: An example from New Guinea. In A. Kleinman & B. Good (Eds.), *Culture and Depression* (pp. 101–133). Berkeley, Calif.: University of California Press.

Sears, D., Peplau, L., Freedman, J., & Taylor, S. (1988). *Social psychology* (6th ed.). Englewood Cliffs, N.J.: Prentice Hall.

Seligman, M. (1988). Boomer blues. *Psychology Today, 22,* 50–55.

Seligman, M. (1989). Explanatory style: Predicting depression, achievement, and health. In M. Yapko (Ed.), *Brief therapy approaches to treating anxiety and depression* (pp. 5–32). New York: Brunner/Mazel.

Seligman, M. (1990). *Learned optimism.* New York: Knopf.

Sherman, S. (1988). Ericksonian psychotherapy and social psychology. In J. Zeig & S. Lankton (Eds.), *Developing Ericksonian therapy* (pp. 59–90). New York: Brunner/Mazel.

Silver, M. (1973). Hypnotherapy as related to repression—sensitization and mood. *American Journal of Clinical Hypnosis, 15,* 245–249.

Skolnick, A. & Skolnick, J. (Eds.), (1986). *Family in transition.* Boston: Little, Brown & Co.

Spiegel, H., & Spiegel, D. (1978). *Trance and treatment: Clinical uses of hypnosis.* New York: Basic Books.

Sundberg, N., Taplin, J., & Tyler, L. (1983). *Introduction to clinical psychology.* Englewood Cliffs, N.J.: Prentice-Hall.

Tavris, C. (1989). *Anger: The misunderstood emotion.* New York: Touchstone.

Terman, S. (1980). Hypnosis and depression. In H. Wain (Ed.), *Clinical hypnosis in medicine* (pp. 201–208). Chicago: Year Book Medical Publishers.

Trad, P. (1986). *Infant depression.* New York: Springer-Verlag.

Walsh, F. (1982). Conceptualizations of normal family functioning. In F. Walsh (Ed.), *Normal family processes.* New York: Guilford Press.

Watkins, J. (1987). *Hypnotherapeutic techniques.* New York: Irvington.

Watzlawick, P. (1978). *The language of change: Elements of therapeutic communication.* New York: Basic Books.

Watzlawick, P. (1982). Erickson's contribution to the interactional view of psychotherapy. In J. Zeig (Ed.), *Ericksonian approaches to hypnosis and psychotherapy* (pp. 147–154). New York: Brunner/Mazel.

Watzlawick, P. (Ed.) (1984). *The invented reality.* New York: Norton.

Watzlawick, P. (1985). Hypnotherapy without trance. In J. Zeig (Ed.), *Ericksonian psychotherapy, Vol. 1: Structures* (pp. 5–14). New York: Brunner/Mazel

Watzlawick, P., Weakland, J., & Fisch, R. (1974). *Change: Principles of problem formation and problem resolution.* New York: New York: Norton.

Weakland, J. (1982). Erickson's contribution to the double bind. In J. Zeig (Ed.), *Ericksonian approaches to hypnosis and psychotherapy* (pp. 169–169). New York: Brunner/Mazel.

Weinstein, N., & Lachendro, E. (1982). Egocentrism as a source of unrealistic optimism. *Personality and Social Psychology Bulletin, 8,* 195–200.

Weissman, M. (1983). Psychotherapy in comparison and in combination with pharmacotherapy for the depressed outpatient. In J. Davis & J. Maas (Eds.), *The affective disorders* (pp. 409–418). Washington, D.C.: American Psychiatric Press.

Weissman, M. (1987). Advances in psychiatric epidemiology: Rates and risks for major depression. *American Journal of Public Health, 77,* 445–451.

Weitzenhoffer, A. (1989). *The practice of hypnotism* (Vol.2). New York: John Wiley & Sons.

Wender, P., & Klein, D. (1981). *Mind, mood, and medicine: A guide to the new biopsychiatry.* New York: Farrar, Straus, & Giroux.

Wetzel, J. (1984). *Clinical handbook of depression.* New York: Gardner Press.

Willner, P. (1985). *Depression: A psychobiological synthesis.* New York: John Wiley & Sons.

Wolberg, L. (1948). *Medical hypnosis.* New York: Grune & Stratton.

Wright, M., & Wright, B. (1987). *Clinical practice of hypnotherapy.* New York: Guilford Press.

Yapko, M. (1983). A comparative analysis of direct and indirect hypnotic communication styles. *American Journal of Clinical Hypnosis, 25,* 270–276.

Yapko, M. (1988). *When living hurts: Directives for treating depression.* New York: Brunner/Mazel.

Yapko, M. (Ed.) (1989). *Brief therapy approaches to treating anxiety and depression.* New York: Brunner/Mazel.

Yapko, M. (1990). *Trancework: An introduction to the practice of clinical hypnosis* (2nd ed.). New York: Brunner/Mazel.

Yapko, M. (1991, May/June). A therapy of hope. *Family Therapy Networker,* 34–39.

Yapko, M. (1992). *Free yourself from depression.* Emmaus, Pa: Rodale Press.

Zeig, J. (Ed.) (1980a). *A teaching seminar with Milton H. Erickson.* New York: Brunner/Mazel.

Zeig, J. (1980b). Symptom prescription techniques: Clinical applications using elements of communication. *American Journal of Clinical Hypnosis, 23,* 23–32.

Zeig, J. (1985). The clinical use of amnesia: Ericksonian methods. In J. Zeig (Ed.), *Ericksonian psychotherapy, Vol. 1: Structures* (pp. 317–337). New York: Brunner/Mazel.

Zeig, J. (1987). Therapeutic patterns of Ericksonian influence communication. In J. Zeig (Ed.), *The evolution of psychotherapy* (pp. 392–406). New York: Brunner/Mazel.

Zeig, J. (1990). Seeding. In J. Zeig & S. Gilligan (Eds.), *Brief therapy: Myths, methods and metaphors* (pp. 221–246). New York: Brunner/Mazel.

Name Index

Subject Index